Not Dead Yet
~
Reflections on Life, Aging & Death

Not Dead Yet

~

Reflections on Life, Aging & Death

Cahaba Press
Eureka Springs
Arkansas
USA

Cahaba Press
483 County Road 231
Eureka Springs, AR 72631
USA
Cahabapress.com

Cover Design by T & T Designs. ttcreative.us

Cover illustration: The Jolly Flatboatmen by George Caleb Bingham. 1846. (PD) Public Domain. The National Gallery of Art, Washington, D.C.

Editor: Sharon Freeman Laborde

ISBN:9781707264438

Printed in the United States of America

Dedication

To Sam Davis: carpenter, craftsman, educator, and artisan. Sam's creativity, kindness, and example inspired this book. He is among those rare human beings who successfully marries mind and body. Thank you, Sam.

Table of Contents

Foreword

Book titles should accurately describe what a book is about and shout *pick me! pick me!* at readers browsing bookstore aisles or going clickity-click through Amazon's hottest Kindle deals. Crafting such a title is hard work, and it was a particularly daunting challenge for the makers of the book in your hand.

Not Dead Yet: Reflections on Life, Aging, and Death generally engages the accuracy obligation: everyone appearing here is still alive (more or less) and each contributor reflects on getting old, on the prospects of dying sooner rather than later, and on what it's like to "be" old in a tech-drenched, sensory overloaded culture focused on young, thin, and rich Wannabes.

The word "generally" in the paragraph above means there is no way to accurately describe old age. "Being" old is, like any other age, a day to day adventure that varies from person to person. The essential difference from other times of life is that old people have experienced 4-years-old, and 14 and 44 and know the answer to the question, "Will you still need me, will you still feed me, when I'm 64?"

More than one of the essayists in *Not Dead Yet* believes "old age" is a state of mind and not a state of being. I'm delighted by these optimists, but balance their *joie de vie* against the time I spend in physician's offices and how my rear-end has traveled to my front-side. Not all old people count the days they have left, but we all count pills.

Who are the essayists in *Not Dead Yet*? Most of us are middleclass twits, to borrow a phrase from Monty Python. We are white people who went to college, earned money and pay taxes, got married and got mortgages, raised families, and worried about our cholesterol levels. In the words of Zorba the Greek, "the whole catastrophe!"

But we're all so much more than that too.

1

Our contributors include a filmmaker and a fine artist, a tired, road weary peddler who earned a million frequent flyer miles, a school teacher from flat Nebraska, and an Arkansas Living Treasure who makes his home in the Ozark Mountains. Our political leanings and religious affiliations are a challenge to any bell curve maker, and most of us have chosen the road not taken; roads that slip into Berlin and Johannesburg in the early morning hours, flow alongside the Mekong River, sidestep into truck stops in Tucumcari, New Mexico, and dead-end in the Black Sea. We've been members of the human race for a long, long time…and for just the blink of an eye.

The diversity of our various backgrounds is reflected in the essays in *Not Dead Yet*. And our diversity certainly complicated our quest for a title. Suggestions ranged from the bleakly comic *Waiting for Snuffman* to the calmly introspective *Everyday Elders: Reflections on Life, Aging and Death*. My own favorite was *Everything I Didn't Learn in Kindergarten*.

Ultimately, *Not Dead Yet* was chosen on the advice of a marketing consultant. He told us short titles sell more books than long titles and, if we hope to attract younger readers, we absolutely must avoid all inferences, however oblique, to the phrase, "When I was your age…"

We have avoided that phrase. Now, please, *pick me! pick me!* and buy our book.

~ Dan Krotz

JIM YOUNG

I Say This About Aging

By

Jim Young

I feel honored to be a contributor to this book on aging even though I don't find age, especially old age, to be a particularly interesting subject. Too many older folks I know speak mostly about their ailments as they age. Not my idea of a fun conversation. Besides, old age isn't some kind of grand prize. As Groucho Marx is to have said: "Anyone can get old. All you have to do is live long enough."

And that's the real issue, isn't it? For the most part, we now live longer than people did a century ago, and we don't quite know what to do about it. Except to do what others tell us to do about it. Which is the downer at hand: *everyone* tells us what to do about it. And, mostly, they make lots of money when we fall prey to their admonitions.

I'll confess my primary viewpoint about age right here at the beginning: I refer to aging as saging; a process, not a thing to be troubled about. No, I didn't say sagging. I said saging, or sageing, if you must—becoming wiser. That is, becoming more aware over time of wisdom being our innate state of Being.

A story to cement the point. Years ago, three of us in Eureka Springs, Arkansas, population around 2200 at the time, initiated a group we had the temerity to name the Arkansas Metaphysical Society: ARMS. How clever of us. Marsha, Carol and I initiated it because we thought that if the three of us enjoyed conversing about matters metaphysical, there surely must be others who would also appreciate the opportunity. The group came about through an open invitation in the local newspaper. Marsha and Carol thought there would be quite a few join us for the founding meeting; I was a bit more skeptical. To my surprise and sheer delight, twenty-eight people showed up that first night. They were mostly middle-aged men and women. I call anyone older than I am middle-aged, so you get the idea.

Anyway, we had splendid conversations on a wide variety of topics over the years, and group trust was high. In no time at all the weekly meetings became a love-in, and we began drawing people from out of town to our sensitive, deeply conversational ways. As moderator for the group, one evening I felt such strong ties to the idea of age and wisdom being related that when it came time to sing happy birthday to one of our esteemed group, I suggested we sing "happy saging," rather than "happy birthday." Of course, this suggestion cemented the group view that I was rather weird, but the idea took ahold of such occasions in a hurry. And I wasn't the only one who enjoyed it.

Okay, I know it was an unusual idea, but if you haven't tried it, don't knock it. After all, when's the last time someone wished you a happy state of wisdom?

Just to be sure about the meaning of saging, I don't mean to suggest that you sage your home by smudging it with a stick of sage to expel "evil spirits," although that's not a bad idea at all. Rather, I mean to feel well and healthy, to heal thoughts to the contrary, and celebrate your real identity as one of wisdom.

Just what is it we must heal, feel better about, and be healthier than? To start with, we need to heal all the false beliefs and opinions about age that we've taken on as our own—as if they are the truth. We can learn to feel better about life and ourselves in general: stop accepting false declarations about age and how we really feel—and can. And recast our lives to implement healthier approaches to daily living, separating ourselves from all the unhealthy habits we've taken on during our life journey.

I know, all this can confuse, rather than simplify. Stick with me for just a moment, though. It'll all become clearer to you. Well, let's be absolutely honest: I hope the idea of age becomes clearer to me, first—so I have a better chance of making it also clearer to you...if I can just remember long enough to do that. ...

Aha, another unfounded aspersion sneaks into the conversation: that as we age, we naturally forget more than we used to. This is possible, of course, but unless you're making your way into Alzheimer's disease, most probably you're forgetting more in the same ways even those far younger are witnessing these days. Just why is this? Because the remarkable degree of everyday distraction and stress in our lives makes it more difficult to remember even the day of the week, or what we had for breakfast. At least the young people I often speak with declare this to be true. So, let's put at least some of this to rest for now.

Besides, experience has shown me that when I seem to have lost an idea I'm speaking about, it turns up to be just around the corner someplace—and it always returns when I let go of the need to find it.

So, here's where I'm coming from. Over the years—and that's 83 of them for me—I've heard what's called old age get a really bad rap. And most of it comes from people who operate mostly from ego consciousness—expressing their opinions and beliefs based primarily on difference and separation. Because others look and behave differently from us, we separate or distance ourselves from them as being some kind of "them" we don't want to identify with. In this case, the "them" is being old. To make matters even worse, we impart additional characteristics to being old that aren't true to validate our limited vision.

For example, a doctor told my late mother-in-law she should exercise more as part of her desire to lose some weight. Sure enough, she went out and purchased a treadmill, and actually tried it—for three…whole…days. While visiting her, not knowing that she had quit her commitment more quickly than she had declared it, I asked her how she was enjoying exercising.

Without hesitation or thought, she replied, "I'm *not* enjoying it!"

"Why not?" I asked. "Something wrong?"

"It's not *something* that's wrong. It's that *everything* is wrong! I'm just too old for this. My body is too sore when I'm finished."

"Mom, you're not sore because you're old. You're sore because you're out of shape. The soreness you feel is because you're starting to flush toxins you've stored up over the years of inactivity. That's a good sign, telling you exercise is beginning to work for you. If you continue, in a very short time you'll flush most or all of the toxins out and you'll feel much better. Of course, you should give your body a rest once or twice a week to give it time to recover. But we all require recovery time, so that too is not a factor of age."

Did the explanation work? Of course not! Her life-long conditioning to the contrary kept her from seeing the truth of the matter. Sad. But true. Certainly, the immense impact of conditioning—domestication, I like to call it—is true for all of us, no matter what age.

I've had to keep a sharp eye on this same culprit, myself, this castigating tongue of age-blaming belief and opinion. Which, thankfully, is partly responsible for turning my focus to one of going inward to hear the voice heard in silence for my answers about such things.

Here's another example of how our misuse of imagination about aging can work against us. Nearly five years ago, I was rear-ended at a stoplight, causing some pretty severe damage to both car and body. After spending nearly $30,000 over three years recovering, I still wasn't back to what I considered normal. Interestingly, it was then that I began hearing myself saying that this was the first time in my life I had felt age.

The fact of the matter, though, was that I hadn't yet given my body the time and proper attention it needed to heal itself. What I was feeling had nothing at all to do with age, but with frustration over setting unrealistic expectations for myself.

As I listened carefully to my body—and returned to an even healthier regimen of exercise, rest and sound nutritional principles—my energy began to pick up and my viewpoint began to sparkle again. Even at that, I'm still not the whole way back to where I'd like to be. But at least I have a good start on it.

It was then I realized, at least temporarily, that I had unwittingly adapted Geoffrey Parfitt's thinking about age: "People say age is just a state of mind. I say it's more about the state of your body." Sounds just like my late mother-in-law.

That was a good thing for me to acknowledge, though, because it caused me to reflect inwardly to see how I really felt about age as I traverse the continuum of life.

Quite suddenly, I began noticing other comments about age...about what it is and is not. I particularly like what Jackie Joyner-Kersee says: "Age is no barrier. It's a limitation put on your mind." And, I'd add, it's just like any belief and opinion is: a limitation we put on ourselves, which only distracts us from looking inward to the truth of it all.

In this very important insight rests the wisdom of Mark Twain: "Age is an issue of mind over matter. If you don't mind, it doesn't matter." And the same can be said for much that troubles us in this life of ours. If we don't mind—it doesn't matter. What someone else thinks about us, for example, is not something to worry about. What others think or say about us says everything about them and nothing at all about us—so what does it really matter?

Let's face it: what we claim to be our age is simply a number we've been told is supposed to be put on us, like counting rings in a tree. It's all made up, out of a need to label. Yet again, as a figment of ego consciousness, its purpose is to make us different from others, so we can judge others through comparison and contrast.

In still another sense, let's consider what is really meant when someone says something like, "Gee, do I have to wait two whole weeks for our vacation to begin?" I can't say what they really mean by their question, except to hear it as a sign of impatience. But, if asked what response I'd make to such a declaration, I'd likely say something like this: "How can that be a long time to wait, when, in the continuum of eternity, two weeks is hardly a blink of a moment." In that framework, two weeks fly by in a flash. So, age, like time, is relative. For the most part, we're only as old as we think we are.

It is true that at 83 I can't do some things I used to do at

23. Well, that's only partially true. I can still do most of them. It only takes me more time to do them—and with a little more care.

It's not age that determines that so much, but the fact that I'm not in the physical, mental and emotional condition I was at 23. Once I come to grips with that understanding, I can refine my commitment to appropriate activities that can reshape my life, using inward discernment about such things to guide me along the way—every day.

At this point in my life, I feel more like Billie Burke, who once said, "Age is of no importance unless you are a cheese." And more like Joan Collins, as well, "Age is just a number. It's totally irrelevant unless, of course, you happen to be a bottle of wine." No wonder I love to indulge myself in such a compelling combination of treats!

I'll close this part of the commentary with a brief story that reflects Terri Guillemet's version of age: "Age attacks us when we least expect it." Confession time: From time to time, I'm still drawn to the allure of feminine beauty, yes even at age 83. I like a woman of authentic beauty but not narcissistic; intellectual but not too literal; light- hearted but not goofy; keen sense of humor but not bawdy; spiritually deep but not evangelical; warm but not mushy; an easy conversationalist but not bombastic; about my age, but who looks and acts younger than that; who's *alive* but not overpowering. I'm sure to have left a few desirable characteristics out, but I'm confident you get the idea. The point is, in such cases, I've been known to invite such a person for a drink or lunch.

Finding myself across the table, with a goal only to engage the potential for finding a new friend to enjoy the theater or symphony with—wanting nothing more than the pleasure of her company—the conversation most always goes something like what follows. "Do tell me something about yourself." Fueled by that single request, we exchange fascinating stories with one another. It feels more and more comfortable in each new moment of now.

Then, the inevitable quest begins in earnest. "Do you have children?" she asks.

"Yes, five of them, all grown now, and living in all parts of the country." (At this point, I want to encourage her to get right to the point, but stay with it to see if this conversation will be any different from past ones.)

"Oh, how old are they?" she rejoins. (This is the real tip that she wants to figure out how old I am.)

So, to be playful about it, I respond with something akin to: "Well, they range from twins at 52 to my oldest who just turned 60, which says that I got married the first time at the age of 10, having our first child when 11." Followed by a momentary pause to accommodate her disbelief. Then, "I'm just kidding, of course. That's my way of saying that while most people don't think I look or act like I'm 83, that's the truth of the matter."

"Oh, age is not a factor for me. Age is a matter of feeling, not one of years," she finishes.

Our conversation continues, enjoyable and nicely revealing, in a good way. When we part, even before I can invite her for another exploratory time together, she inserts that she'll be in touch soon. So far—it hasn't happened. It has never happened. Not even once. So much for age not being a factor.

Upon reflection, I wasn't quite honest about no one every responding favorably in such circumstances. I once had a relationship with a lovely woman a bit younger than I was at the time. For a while, she reinforced the idea that she didn't have any difficulty with our age difference. Then, one morning, she woke up and realized that later in life she might end up having to care for an elderly man, her life partner. Imagine that! It didn't take but a split second for her to ditch our relationship—and then blame it on me. It is what it is, neither more nor less; neither right nor wrong. I look at it this way: better sooner than later.

Nevertheless, "age attacks us when we least expect it." And bites us on the behind. Or, is it how some see age that bites us so hard? Or—could it simply be that I'm just too darn picky? Ya' think?

On the other hand, particularly in the past ten years or so, I've had some lovely conversations with a number of young people, mostly servers in restaurants. Over time, getting to know some of the staff around town pretty well, I've been blessed by quite a few who've become like family. What's even more amazing is how personal the conversations can become. To top it off, it has become really personal with about 6-8 of them. And it's always they who initiate a particular line of questioning. It's usually gone like this:

"Jim, do you have grandchildren?"

"Yes, I have, seven. Why do you ask?

"Because, I've never met a grandfather on either side of our family."

"And?"

"And, I'd like to ask if you'd be my surrogate grandfather."

B L O W N   A W A Y!

"You *bet* I will!"

Now I have as many surrogate grandchildren as I do biological ones. What a fortunate man I am. And I'm extremely glad I'm old enough to be a designated grandfather.

What tickles my funny bone most is the names they come to call me: Gramps; Grandpa; Pops, Papoú, Papa—on it goes. And each greeting is always accompanied by a welcoming hug. How much better could it be? Young people today have *such* good judgment!

So, here's how I *now* feel about age. The other day, when on one of my several-mile walks in the neighborhood, I suddenly realized, "For the most part, I'm not really feeling age. The better shape I get in, the less I feel age at all." On an even deeper level, I feel that my *body* may now be somewhat different, but the real "I," the "I" that hears all these declarations, is as ageless and as priceless as it is eternal.

In a way, it's like saying, "I'm *not* fat. I *have* fat." "I'm *not* a hemorrhoid. I *have* hemorrhoids." (I don't really!) In this case, "*I'm* not age. My body—my body of *thought* about age—is merely changing." As long as I don't identify with either my body or age, I'm home free. And perfectly at home living true to what I *really* am: Life eternal.

At this point, I identify most closely with Ralph B. Perry, who was to have said, "Age should not have its face lifted, but it should rather teach the world to admire wrinkles as the etchings of experience and the firm line of character." Which is akin to the Persian poet, Rumi: "Let the soul of man be revealed in the character of his face." Try living embraced by such attitudes and see where they get you.

Before closing this down, I want to share a single gripe about aging. Just one? Yep. Just one. Actually, it's not a gripe about aging itself, but about the pharmaceutical industry, which offends and assaults both our intelligence and life space with untold numbers of ads on TV and on other social frameworks. Mostly, the ads refer to meds they make up for conditions that we make up, focusing attention on some need for a quick fix of a kind. At this count, the stress-producing and life-limiting bombardment amounts to roughly 50% of TV ads, and they perpetrate and perpetuate a focus on what "appears to be" our unhealthy status as humans. Heck, just a short time ago they even advertised a drug to "cure" a bend in a fellow's thingy—when the real cure is to stop one's dependence on—or fascination with—Cialis or Viagra, both highly stressful to that part of a man's physique. Of *course,* it *would* bend under extreme stress!

Funny thing is, you won't find such ads on European TV. No wonder they're relatively saner and live so much longer than we do!

But I don't worry about all this any longer. Gratefully, I've learned that all I really need to get over such distractions is a slight change of attitude—and to turn off the TV! Another idea just came up as a way that could also help. Since birth, my name has been James Young. Seeing as I'm still young at heart and enjoy setting my inner child free, I think I'll give serious thought to changing my first name from Jim to Forever. What do you think?

In the end, it's all pretty simple. Just be the sage you most definitely—and *already*—are. And forget what anyone else may think or say about you when you do. *That* is absolutely *none* of your business! Not minding is one of the *ultimate* benefits of aging. How very wise!

Jim Young After serving nearly thirty years in various aspects of higher education, Dr. James H. Young currently is a published spiritual author and program presenter, and a widely collected documentary/fine art photographer. He has served with distinction as a teacher, distinguished professor of higher education, and in a variety of leadership positions, including President of State University of New York at Potsdam and Chancellor of the University of Arkansas at Little Rock. Dr. Young is a graduate of the ecumenical School for Spiritual Directors at the Pecos Benedictine Monastery (NM), and served as the monastery's first lay director of public relations and fund-raising, where he initiated an extensive religious arts program. Jim is co-founder and facilitator of the Arkansas Metaphysical Society in Eureka Springs, AR, and The Aristotle Group in Hot Springs, AR, where he also served as the Minister Emeritus of the Creative Life Church (New Thought).

A featured contributing author to *PlanetLightworker* and *The Reki Times*, spiritual monthly E-journals, Jim has received awards for spiritual poetry and prose, as well as for photographic images appearing in juried exhibitions worldwide. Young faithfully follows his inner calling by writing about and leading others from various religious and spiritual traditions to the deeper, life-changing meaning and purpose for them. Jim's writings, presentations and teachings re-frame Life's journey: from one of separation and the chaos separation engenders, across the spiritual threshold to Oneness, and the inner joy and peace that witness this perspective. Author of 25 spiritual books, Dr. Young is a gifted inspirational speaker who often uses Life's stories to convey spiritual meaning, and inspires others to look within for the Truth that transcends the superficial.

Mary Woodard

I See Dead People

By

Mary Woodard

I've been thinking about what it is like to become old. Although still on the cusp, I would like to describe the landscape. I see dead people. They are everywhere, and they bring richness to the tapestry woven.

I do not mean to imply that I am psychic or deranged. I learned that people died and you couldn't play with them anymore when I was five and Great-aunt Allene died. Susan and I ran crying into our bedroom to throw our faces into our pillow and weep. Dead was a state to avoid becoming, and we were sad when it happened to those we loved. These many years later, however, Allene's ring is on my finger. I remember the snow that fell endlessly across her television screen and the patterned concrete of her sidewalk where I jumped rope. She taught sixth grade and sometimes so do I.

Youth is a rollercoaster: jubilance and sorrow; hope and utter despair. Age erodes the cliffs and smooths the rocky paths. It is almost like a microscope that was focused on cells in an onionskin has been adjusted, and now it is a cell, a seed, and the cheese and onion pie that my sister Ann made for my first wedding.

At dinner my cousin Jimmy seems to be at the next table. I remember the stroke Jimmy had. Compression sleeves encouraged slagging circulation. Jimmy died, but I see him at the adjacent table and want to stop to give greetings. He must be a good man with humor on the tip of his tongue that never offends. Praises are raised for Jimmy and the man whose resemblance has called him to my mind.

On the night my first husband died, my mind stayed awake all night, staring at the hanging body that the EMT's unbolted. Hearing is the last sense remaining for those dying. I feared that I may have screamed or made a guttural moan he may have heard. I opened all the windows and counted blessings. I showed him in all ways that love is not something that is mutated by moments. I hear his laughter still. Unfathomable sorrow and exquisite joy comingled.

I teach students in a public middle school. They sometimes ask me about my life and sometimes they don't and I tell them anyway. I tell them about stubbing my toe at Al Gaston's swimming pool when I was three and how my sister Susan and Cousin Betsy helped me hobble to our cabin for a bandage before the sharks could smell my blood and come to eat me. Students ask me how I can remember events from such distant times. Maybe old age just gives me a bigger collection of moments to recall.

I was eighteen when my father died in the hospital. I was in my class at the University. A voracious reader with a good vocabulary, I knew the word "keening" but that day I learned with my heart. Walking through the glade of pines to my car, my sorrow pouring out, caught by birds and carried off, a grief I was too weak to bear broke me open, and I keened.

I saw him in the hospital. His eyes had been closed but his mouth hung open, and I could see how hard he had fought the cancer to stay in his life for us. I still hear his laughter and take his counsel. He left his spent shell in that hospital, but he is everywhere I go. I even catch myself remembering him being present at events that took place after his death.

And some days my hand covers my mouth, holding my soul captive in my corporal form. Becoming old is accepting that some days are like that.

So I suppose age gives me some perspective. The people I meet for a moment can be eternal if the contact imprints and alters me.

My husband says old age sucks. He says this because his back has been in spasm, and he is tired of responding to dire emergencies that are not dire but merely require patience and perspective. His patience for impatience is worn thin.

I can converse with great personal knowledge about cellulite, plantar fasciitis, deafness, cataracts, and many physical ailments. When I look in the mirror, however, I am frequently shocked. My mother told me this happened to her all the time, so it came as no surprise. I walk around, certain that I look like I did when I was twenty. Then I see my reflection and wonder where that old woman came from. My sister Ann was ten years older than me, so I usually just thought it was Ann, but Ann started showing the symptoms of Multiple Systems Atrophy when she was about my age. I stopped seeing her in my mirror when she died. Now I just catch glimpses of strangers who I mistake for Ann. They are always so beautiful and helpful.

Ann told me that she met an angel in the aisles of a Lowes. She was shopping on her own and needed something off a shelf. Ann's disease had progressed to the point where her neck could no longer support her head, so a man, Ann's angel, offered assistance. He asked about her condition and asked permission to pray with her. There in the aisles of Lowes they cried together, prayed, and released past angers and resentments. That is one thing I

21

remember about the angels in the Bible. They all start out by saying, "Don't be afraid."

Ann wasn't afraid and neither was Susan. The day before she died Sue said, "I've got this." She battled pancreatic cancer with great fortitude for more than eighteen months. Then we kept her on the regular dose of morphine as she asked.

They weren't afraid, but they certainly wanted to live. Both my sisters were artists, wives, mothers, grandmothers, and great friends. They live in so many moments.

I have witnessed the close of so many days that craved no sequel. Grief is like finding that the end of a highway is a brick wall. We collide and feel convinced that the journey is over. Night falls; we take our rest, and the relentless morning comes. We may believe that the wrenching pain of loss is unbearable, but we would be wrong. The sun rises even if we order it to cease.

I think the universe is much larger than known science suspects. More timelines than just the fragile thread we tread, splinter, and divide with each "what if." In grief I once asked God to take me away from the timeline I was on. I said I was too tired and too broken and wanted to move to a happier place. On that night I dreamt an emergency called me to the hospital to see my daughter. At the nurse's station I was asked, "How old is your daughter." I said, "She is three. No, she is seven. No, she is twelve." And as I gave those answers I knew all the answers were true. On some other timeline, built with other what ifs, other joys and other sorrows would greet me. So I stayed and am glad I did. Since then I have celebrated weddings, births, and millions of miracles that could never had occurred on any of the timelines that had not included that grief. Love creates miracles, life blossoms, in the most unexpected times and places.

We are made in the image of God and co-create our sense of self. Using the world around us as our medium, we build and carve. That may be why I feel such comfort in being on the cusp of seniority: I find my form familiar.

Who will author our lives if we fail to do the task ourselves? Unless we author our lives we will be peripheral characters. I do not mind being peripheral. One thing age has taught me is the richness of the stories untold.

God spoke clearly to me once. I was deep in prayer. Young, maybe twelve, I prayed for peace and the end to the conflict in Vietnam. I used words that I thought God would find eloquent and worthy of response. I heard God clearly.

He said, "Shut up."

It must have been God because no one else—not even my imagination—would be so rude. The crude tone told me that I should devote more time to listening than to speaking. My dear Lord, I hope you know that I have tried.

I see so many dead people. I see Fletcher tipping his chair, pretending to read. He sits in the corner of my classroom as his brother and I play cards. I see Jennifer in a canoe and we row and talk under the cloudless sky. And the boyfriend who would ask her to kneel and look away as he shot her in the back of the head would be far away, straying down a path that tried to hide from love and faith and all that binds us.

So perhaps the time has come to use my voice, to author my story.

I recall the rollercoaster of youth. Intimacy of moments is more compelling than sage distance. Do I use the voice of age or the urgency of youth?

As an older woman I can select the tools I will use. I can select my perspective. I can craft the resources provided by life. I see dead people because they live within me. I am blind and deaf because they go beyond my ken. I can speak because I have been touched by moments I can never control.

Mary Woodard teaches in a public middle school in Lincoln, Nebraska. She is the youngest child and youngest cousin in her family, so many of her memories are of events that took place before her birth. She is a wife, a mom, a grandmother, and a Sunday School teacher.

Doug Stowe

Not as Old as Dirt

By

Doug Stowe

I first began to notice I was old when a few young, polite men started showing a bit of deference to me as I entered or exited the grocery store. Whether it was that they were taught to be kind and respectful to their elders or that they'd observed that compared to me they have all the time in the world, I'll not pretend to know. We do reach a certain point when however hard and fast we hold to the lies our projected image of self can tell, the truth of what we see in the mirror overrides the fictions we want to believe in.

It's funny being old doesn't feel so old on the inside. I'm still the same young guy observing what surrounds me and attempting to make sense of it all. I do nap … a thing I'd avoided since Kindergarten. In fact, I can fall asleep at the touch of a button, and the keyboard at this computer has its way of luring me into sleep…

… much later.

Oh, yes. Where was I? Being old is not the same as getting old. Getting old is the thing that scares the daylights out of the young, but once it creeps up on you, there's no going back. It's either old or dead. In 2009 the Arkansas Arts Council and Department of Heritage named me a living treasure for the state. The good part of being named a treasure is "living." A friend, Jimmy Fliss noted, "It's better than being buried," so that's what I tell my friends when they ask.

So let's get on with this while I still have time. There's one thing that old folks talk about that young folks rarely bother with. That's health. Most of us are troubled with minor annoyances. Most men dribble inappropriately when we get to a certain age, and I do not mean basketball. So if hanging out with a bunch of old men, do an experiment. Count the minutes before the subject of prostate comes up.

One thing I've noticed about being old is that I spend much less time hurrying around doing nothing. I've gotten smarter about my work so it takes less effort. A woodworking friend of mine, Jerry Forshee, called me parsimonious. He meant it as a compliment: that I've learned to cut out a lot of unnecessary steps; so while employers, not knowing any better, might think a young whippersnapper was doing a lot because of the motion blur of his or her moving around the workplace, old folks tend to cut out many of the unnecessary motions that make you unproductive and prone to catastrophic mistakes. Failure to recognize the value of older workers is particularly a problem when the employer is a whippersnapper him or herself, and there's a lot of that.

We old folks may have earned a bad rep for moving slowly, when in fact, we may move smart. At the Marc Adams School of Woodworking, a good friend Zane would tell new students, "You'd better hurry up and get it done so you'll have time to go back and fix it." This does not mean we old folks don't make mistakes or even the same mistakes over and over; but we still, in balance, and even with an allowance for naps, can outperform.

I've been a woodworker for the last 45 years and learned

a few things. The first is that no craftsman works in complete isolation. We are bound to the will and wishes of customers. We are bound also to the will of the wood. It will do only certain things. It will bend only under heat and stress. It has grain that determines how individual species and individual pieces of it can be best used. Even when we are alone in our wood shops, facets of human culture intrude. We look at shapes and lines and wonder, is that right? We look at the sanding marks or misfit joints and wonder if our customers will notice and condemn. And to make a very long story short, no man, woman, child, or maker of useful beauty is an island unto himself.

Chaucer wrote: "The lyf short, and the craft so longe to lerne." And boy howdy was he right. Accepting wood as one's teacher is something that can go on for a very long time. And once you've accepted wood as your teacher, getting it to accept you back and bend to your will can take even longer.

Jean Jacques Rousseau, 18th century French philosopher, had said that if you put a young man in a wood shop, his hands will work to the benefit of his brain, and he'll become a philosopher while thinking himself only a craftsman. And so there are things you learn about life from woodworking, not the least or last of which is: We make mistakes. Things go haywire, and if we've not yet mastered the art of self-forgiveness they can knock you on your heels for a while, even to the point where you won't get up. There's also a bit of humility involved. Think you're hot shit? In woodworking the shit hits the fan almost exactly at that very moment when you begin to think you're hot. Real wood tolerates no pretense, and while it demands our attention it simultaneously forces us to think about bigger things.[1]

Another thing you can learn from woodworking is that things tend to work out best when we start with a plan. It might be a full-blown SketchUp 3-D illustration showing expanded views and dimensions of each and every part, or it can be as simple as a quick sketch on a napkin or on the end of a board. Nevertheless, in order to make beautiful and useful things, they turn out best when they start with a plan. Of course, plans go awry. That's another place where forgiveness comes in handy. You've heard of plan A, and then of plan B, and from there we can run through the whole alphabet and still not exhaust the need for planning and re-planning. As a younger man I tried to do very complex and challenging things: carving, inlay, veneering hand-cut dovetails, whole rooms full of my work. As an old guy I've tried to simplify. I keep telling myself, KISS. Keep things (it) simple smartass. Simple work can be expeditiously done, to greater short-term satisfaction, a thing that matters when you no longer have all the time in the world. Note, the idea of a plan will show up later in this wandering discourse. *(Foreshadowing here)*

And so this brings me to the elephant in the room, and I'm thinking that not all folks reading this are over the hill

---

[1] President Jimmy Carter was the only American President in the last century that was also a woodworker. A good one at that! He brought solar panels to the White House, urged Americans to conserve and insisted we cut back on foreign oil. He was too far ahead of his times, and being a Christian Sunday School teacher, he had no notion of how ugly things would get in bringing his defeat. According to the New York Times, the Reagan campaign plotted with the Iranian Revolutionary Guard to prevent the release of hostages until after the election, thus assuring Carter's defeat. Some say good men don't make good presidents, but if more Americans were woodworkers we'd do a better job of selecting them.

yet. D.E.A.T. H. My daughter asked one time where my father was, and when I told her he was dead, she informed me that she was far too young for that subject. Perhaps she was right. But when a younger sister died recently, a friend of my wife suggested that dying was a teachable moment... in which we learned something about life. And so she's right. A very slightly older cousin told me that as he's gotten older, he's understood less about life and death, and I wonder if he's been barking up the wrong profession. Woodworking might have helped him to get a grasp. After all, what we work with came from dead trees. That leads to another point that I'll make later on in this ramble.

The thing about wood that appeals to those craftsmen who've visited museums is that those things we make to be both useful and beautiful can last far beyond the confines of our own lives. A favorite museum that I like to visit in New York City is the Cloisters. There you find woodwork from the 11th century and before. Can you believe it? Nine hundred year old wooden things: Chests that have held their form even though crafted only with the simple tools available at the time and then thrown about willy-nilly for generations, Religious triptychs, that open to scenes of holy significance, Carvings of famous historic religious figures and much more. Another favorite museum of mine is the Nelson-Atkins Museum in Kansas City where they have a statue of Quan Yin over a thousand years old. In a secret compartment, curators found a scroll containing the names and signatures of the men who carved it. And so to realize that something you make can outlive you, even for generations, or even for centuries, if crafted with love and not simple expedience, makes you think about your own work and may lead to thoughts about what's inevitable but that was too complex an issue for my daughter's young

31

mind.

"Things men have made with wakened hands, and put soft life into are awake through years with transferred touch, and go on glowing for long years. And for this reason, some old things are lovely warm still with the life of forgotten men who made them."

~D.H. Lawrence

Do you look at death or at life in the same way when so much of your life has been poured into the making of things that have the potential to far outdistance your own life? And so I mentioned dead trees. One of the things that woodworkers learn (most likely the hard way) is that wood is never dead. Even that thousand-year-old Quan Yin breathes in and out in response to changes in atmospheric humidity, causing it to expand and contract in thickness and in width over its many years of life in functional form. Wood does not, however, expand or contract in length, the secrets of which are bound in the cellular structure almost invisible to the naked eye. The fact that wood acts as though it's alive, by expanding and contracting but not the same in all directions, makes it particularly confounding to beginning woodworkers. It's also the reason that we have a variety of important woodworking joints and joinery techniques. It's never as simple as one would hope. And so in order to be successful at it, creating pieces that last generations, you must get deeply involved in understanding it. And no two species are exactly the same when it comes to how they will react. Did I mention forgiveness? And so we think that woodworkers work with dead wood? What does dead really mean anyway?

It's funny how a dripping faucet can be heard from three

rooms away. When I lived in Memphis as a young adult, I would take my dog Allie out to Shelby Forest and watch the Mississippi River flow by with such silence that one could hear voices of fishermen a mile away on the other side. In art we are taught about positive and negative space. The positive space is confined within the lines drawn for visual convenience in the portrayal of the object. The negative space is that captured between objects and shapes. Negative space is not empty space. It's like the river. Aside from the water it's filled with the sound of voices from the other side. There are thoughts there. There are relationships, noticed and unnoticed. And within us we have the capacity to shift channels, focusing either on the separate shapes (one of which we self-identify and defend as me), or we can learn to focus upon the relationships that form the interconnectedness between all things. So here's a simple suggestion: Those who have self-identified within the narrow confines of their own bodies to the exclusion of all else have very good reasons to fear death. It's likely their end. For those who direct their love in trust toward all others will stand in the light of eternal life. It may not have anything to do with the attempted consolations offered by religions. It may not even be true in the very long term of things. But as a maker of wood things, and as one who attempts to make them both useful and beautiful and meaningful as well, perhaps it offers some hope or it's the best I can hope for. (Whether anything I've made will last centuries or even decades is for others to decide)

As young folks we are of necessity trapped within the confines of our own bodies. Our bodies demand our attention and if we don't give it to them and attract the attention of others toward fulfilling our needs, we may not survive. Bodies are hungry. They need food, air, light, water, caregivers and actualization. If we do not get those things we're dead. But then there's growth.

A Unitarian Universalist minister Robert Fulghum wrote a classic book entitled *All I Really Need to Know, I Learned in Kindergarten.* But kids won't learn those things in Kindergarten now. Most people these days no longer know where the name Kindergarten came from or what's special about it. They'll know nothing about Friedrich Frobel or his contributions to education. In fact, many educators these days refer to Kindergarten as the new first grade, as it is not any longer the place where kids learn by play to be responsible and thoughtful and to get along with each other. The "new first grade" is where teachers attempt to give them a leg up on reading, math, and standardized testing. In his invention of Kindergarten Froebel had other very important things in mind and is no doubt in a face-plant under-grave rollover at this point in history.

Froebel was walking across a mountain pass in Germany. To his friends he seemed deep in thought, as one can find oneself while on a mountain trail with friends. Suddenly he declared, "Eureka!"[2] (That's the Greek word for Wow! I've just discovered something remarkable). "I know what to call my youngest child! Kindergarten!" he proclaimed. And, of course Kindergarten meant a garden of children and the idea was that children were to grow from within, trusting the same inherent nature that was found within each of the living things in God's creation, including every flower, you and me (and let's not forget trees). And, of

---

[2] Eureka is also the name of my adopted hometown of Eureka Springs, Arkansas. Nearly everyone who arrives here at some point in their lives has some sense of having discovered it, so the name fits. The locals from the backwoods called it Urika.

course the purpose of Kindergarten was not to teach children about death, but about life, and life can only be fully understood by making allowances for the inevitable. (Think plants, gardens, gerbils and guinea pigs here, OK? And let's not forget wood).[3]

Froebel had lost his mother while an infant and when his father had remarried the young woman had at first showered her love on him. That lasted until she had a child of her own at which point Froebel, hardly more than a toddler, was virtually abandoned. He was later farmed off to an uncle who found work for him as a forester's apprentice where he learned the wonders of nature, of the miracle of life, of crafting and of the seasons. Through eyes of longing he observed young mothers with their children, and he noticed the ways in which children were brought gently and gradually to their place within the human race, and much later, as a teacher, Froebel had become concerned with using natural methods through which children would be led toward a sense of interconnectedness and wholeness within the worlds of man and nature. He was accused of being pantheistic, meaning he saw the workings of God in all things. (Was that such a bad thing?) And Kindergarten (a truly amazing thing) was his gift to the world.

---

[3] One of the things that happens with some regularity in the Clear Spring School wood shop where I teach children K-12 how to do woodworking, is that some animal in student care will die and need a coffin to be made. We've made coffins for and held solemn ceremonies for mice, guinea pigs, gerbils, toads, salamanders and lizards. So far no snakes, but what a long box that would take. The children make the box to fit, then line it with leaves, dig a hole, sing together in the high clear voices of early childhood and take turns saying solemn words of praise to the freshly departed.

As the son of a Kindergarten teacher, I regard it as tragic that the original purpose of Froebel's Kindergarten has been abandoned in American Schooling. By learning about life, we also learn about death and may be thereby better prepared for it when it comes to be our turn, as it will.

An old friend of mine Virginia Carey[4] told me a story that if she'd taken the time to tell had enough importance that it was meant to be passed on. No moment between us was wasted. As a young bride and having left high society life in a southern city, she and her first husband bought a small homestead in Gilbert, Arkansas near the Buffalo River. She began noticing that her few precious objects from her high society life were going missing. She asked a neighbor and the neighbor assured her, "What you bring here is ourn, and what you make while you're here is yourn." Modern folks would suggest her stuff had been stolen. Virginia told the story to me, not only because it was an unusual rationalization for theft, but also because it describes what it can take to fit into the fabric of small town life. You must be willing to give yourself fully. Folks know when you're holding back. The same is true of life. It also knows when

---

[4] I met Virginia Carey while I lived in a basement apartment at 1 Ridgeway in Eureka Springs. We had been sitting under a catalpa tree at the Coney stand where the flat iron building is now, and fell into conversation. We became fast friends despite the fact that she was over 50 years older than I. It is said that she planned her own death on Halloween night, 1978. She lived in a house on Spring St. with about 22 steep stone steps and with a heart condition she said that going up and down those steps was keeping her alive. On that Halloween night, she decided to rearrange the furnishings in her home by herself, deliberately pushing her heart beyond its breaking point. Some die suddenly before it would seem to be their time. Others are brought to death almost on a prayer. Those who really love the world that surrounds them may find nothing to fear.

you're holding back. And being better prepared for death demands that we not hold back from life.

Some folks talk about the "fabric" of community. There's a type of pioneer fabric made of linen warp and wool weft that's called "Linsey-Woolsey". It gets its strength from the linen thread and its warmth from wool, and it can take a person years to be woven into the fabric of community life. Some folks are warm, some folks offer strength. Some lucky ones do both and find themselves woven in so effectively that by the time they're ready to be gone replacements are already being woven in. An interesting thing about Linsey-Woolsey is that it can be repaired through a process called "felting." In the process, a bit of wool is laid flat over a hole and with a sharp barbed needle poking again and again hundreds of times, the wool fibers in the patch are tightly entangled in the underlying wool.

So many folks these days think so much of themselves and move around without anchor. Can they but hope to be more than a temporary patch on the fabric of community life, one that can be sloughed off when they are no longer present? It can take years to weasel and weave one's way deeply into things. All that poking can hurt some and many avoid it like the plague.

I'm reminded of a story from Zen. The master was dying and his disciples were gathered round him pleading, "Please master! Please don't leave us!" The master asked, "Where do you think I'd go?" And this brings me to a simple point. To dwell upon one's own individuality rather than upon the needs of those who surround you is a painful path. To ease the path through both life and death requires that we change channels from one that looks exclusively at self and look toward the needs and concerns of others. To do that is an art that requires practice, and it's best to start at an early age. If the strongest part of your self-identity is to be of service to others and to love, perhaps there is no death. The Zen master was so deeply self-entangled into his community that to cease to be there in body was of no importance.

That's why I teach woodworking. I teach it at the Clear Spring School, and at craft schools and for clubs. I write about woodworking, which is also a form of teaching. I do woodworking, which is also a bit about teaching in that I use woods that are intended to instruct others on the beauty and diversity of forest life. With kids, I see their sparks of creativity equaling my own. They love woodworking, just as I was made to love it at an early age. It brings me joy to be witness of their joy. With adults I witness an expansion of their skills and understanding. That understanding is not just about wood, but also about life itself. Some of my students are older than I. In fact, one was 96 and still teaching naval propulsion engineering, and so it's advisable from my perspective to prepare for death by joining the living in ways that serve beyond oneself.

In the early 2000's I became fascinated by a system of Woodworking education from Sweden called Educational Sloyd. I visited the home and gravesite of one of its founders. Otto Salomon had kept a stone from Pestalozzi's[5] grave site on his desk, and I keep a couple from Salomon's on mine. His grave marker was engraved as follows. *Den*

---

[5] Johann Pestalozzi was an early progressive educator whose book "How Gertrude Teaches Her Children" was a best seller in Europe of his time. He had profound influence on Froebel and early educational philosophy. He was noted for his kind demeanor and profound love of children, even those of the poor that the rest of Europe was willing to abandon.

gode är en makt även i graven. Or "the good is a power even in the grave." Let's hope that may be the case.

So at this point in my wandering narration, I want to get to the point. It's my plan to direct my readers to form a plan, a simple plan like that drawn on the end of a board. Get to know those beings (including the plants and animals) that surround you and are part of your own life. Realize that the most self-destructive of human illusions is that of our individuality. We are not alone. We are never separate from each other. Tune in to the "negative" not so empty space that surrounds us and feel the vibes of interconnectedness. Dwell upon them. Not to the point that you drive your truck off a cliff, but so that when you pass, you will do so with grace and style and as a gift to all that surrounds you.

Physicists theorized and proved the concept of cosmic entanglement. Once two particles have been introduced to each other, they can be separated at the furthest corners of the known universe and what is done to one is known by the other and has measurable effect. If that is true, think how entangled we are with each other and with this lovely thing we call life and offer simple trust. Allow yourself to become entangled so deeply into the fabric of community that you are inseparable from it.

Getting engaged in a small community like mine offers special benefits of entanglement. This is not particularly true if you're a mean son of a bitch. Mean SOBs can live anywhere and be as mean as they like. But if you are a kind and caring person, no miser in the distribution of humility and gratitude, you'll find yourself worked in to the point that wherever you go, you find yourself among friends.

Yesterday I went to the carwash to clean my truck. I watched as an older guy washed his motorcycle. He was

meticulous as if he'd no care in the world but for that fat
shiny red bike. When the washer stopped, (it must have
been two dozen quarters by then) he got rags out from the
side compartment and began to slowly, carefully,
meticulously dry and polish his pride and joy. I waited
patiently for him to finish and move on. Not wanting to
appear impatient and rude I went to the coin-operated
vacuum to clean the inside of the truck. After the inside of
my truck was clean he was still polishing and polishing and
it went on and on even though it had to be apparent to him
that there were others including myself waiting in line. We
have choices of whom to be or of whom to become. And I
find comfort in those young men granting me the
consideration given to old men at the entry and exit at the
grocery store.[6] They suggest that world is not all a flat-out
selfish, self-absorbed place. In other words, there's hope
for us all

---

[6] If you live in Eureka Springs, Arkansas, you'll no doubt find your
way to Harts Grocery store. It's been a kind of run-down place for the
last 40 years but serves as a social center. You'll run in for a quick stick
of butter and find yourself pulled in to social entanglements. You'll
find the same thing happening in small neighborhoods in large cities
across the US. To reap the benefits of entanglement requires two
things. 1. That you be open to kindly relations. 2. That you stick to your
small place and attend regularly to the opportunities to reach greater
depth.

Doug Stowe has been a craft artist in Eureka Springs, Arkansas since the fall of 1975. He's the author of 13 books and over 90 magazine articles on woodworking and woodworking education. He has written the blog, Wisdom of the Hands since 2006. He is the father of Lucy Stowe, now living in New York City, and resides with his wife Jean on a wooded hillside at the edge of Eureka Springs. He is a passionate woodworker, an ardent environmentalist, and a staunch advocate for hands-on learning. He was the founder of the Eureka Springs Guild of Artists and Craftspeople in 1977 and was one of three founders of the Eureka Springs School of the Arts in 1998. In semi-retirement, he continues to teach at the Clear Spring School in the program he founded, the "wisdom of the hands," intended to put the hands at the center of learning. His most recent book is the Wisdom of the Hands Guide to Woodworking with Kids.

Don Soderberg

Young and Old

By

Don Soderberg

We heard three short taps of a horn as Mom glanced at the kitchen clock and said, "That will be your grandfather coming over for his Saturday morning coffee—right on time as usual," as she reached for the coffee pot to brew a fresh batch. "That sounded pretty far off. He must be coming up the back lane this morning."

I walked out on the porch to wait for him, but it seemed to take so long I began to think Mom might have been mistaken. I was about to go back in when his truck came around the corner of the barn and pulled up to the house. Every time I see that truck I wonder why anyone would paint a pickup truck green. Red or black sure, but bright green just doesn't seem right. But that was my Gramps. Anyway, I was glad to see him and hollered our standard greeting as he got out of the truck.

"How you doing this morning, Jaime," he said as he came up on the porch. "Do you suppose there's any coffee available around here this morning?"

"Mom's working on it, but I almost gave up waiting on you. It seemed to take a long time from when we heard your horn. Did you stop for a nap along the way?

"No, just stopped for moment with a friend. You know the tree that got hit by lightning a few years ago down along the lane. Well, there's an old red-tailed hawk that sits in what's left of it every morning I come out here, around

45

this time. I don't know if he's finished his breakfast already, or if he's just surveying his turf. But he always sits up there looking around. I kind of think he's waiting for me. So, I always stop and roll down the window, and we just sit and contemplate one another for few minutes. I'm afraid one of these days I'll come by and he won't be there anymore. I do believe I'll miss him when that happens."

"So, it's just two old birds having a senior moment together."

Gramps seemed a bit annoyed with that as I heard him say, "Well, I suppose that's what I should expect from a wise-ass college kid."

"Is there more to it than that?" I asked sheepishly.

"Yeah, quite a bit."

"Are you going to enlighten me?" I asked.

"Don't think you're old enough," he said, opening the door to the kitchen. "Margie, is that coffee ready yet?"

"Coming right up, what were you two jawing about out there?"

Gramps sat down with his coffee and grumbling a bit said, "Oh, it was just an old duffer and a kid who couldn't agree on the state of the world ... I suppose you're pretty busy around here with farming and getting ready to send the kid back to school. Is it even possible you'd have a piece of pie to go with this coffee, what with all the wolves you're feeding around here?"

Mom bristled a bit too as she said, "As near impossible as it is, you know I always save some pie for you. And, for what it's worth, Jaime is hardly a kid anymore. Are you on that old age kick again or is something else making you so cranky this morning?"

"Oh, I guess if I think about it, I'm more worried about an old friend than I would have thought. Time just sort of creeps up on you and gives you pause once in a while to wonder about your own future. But I came out here hoping someone might want to go fishing with me."

"Well, Gramps, I'd love to go fishing with you," I said.

"Think your folks can spare you for a while?

"Sure," I said. "Even teenage manure haulers get a day off once in a while."

Gramps chuckled. "Still thinking like a teenager—didn't you blow out twenty candles on a birthday cake a few weeks ago?"

"Yes, I did!"

So, Gramps went on. "Then I guess you aren't a teenager anymore—end of that excuse for crazy behavior."

Now I had to respond. "Okay, so I'm not a teenager any longer, but I guess you're getting older too. When did that start happening?"

Then Gramps settled in. "Good question—you may turn into a worthy opponent yet. It is kind of funny. Old age just sort of creeps up on you without any formal announcement. The first time it really caught my attention was some years ago when a young girl, maybe not even a teenager, opened a door at McDonald's and held it for me to walk through. I was dumbfounded. I just stood there for a bit trying to figure out what was wrong with that situation. Then I finally walked through and mumbled a *Thank You* ... at least I hope I was polite. She just smiled and went on her way with her friends.

"It took me a while to come to the realization that my outward appearance must convey an older impression than the internal picture I have of myself.

"That little scenario didn't take more than a few seconds, but it might as well have been a formal announcement that I was getting old. It sure made a lasting impression on me.

47

"But, if you look at the first part of life, the march is pretty well defined. You know that at first you start out as a kid. That lasts for thirteen years; then one night you go to bed as a twelve-year-old kid and wake up as a teenager. You get to wear that label for seven years. Then again you go to bed one night and the next morning you wake up and your twenty—like you now Jamie. But you're not an adult for another year. You're caught between—you're a TWEENDER. Then one morning—mark it on the calendar—you wake up and you're twenty-one years old. Officially an adult—now you can legally drink the beer you've been hiding in the barn. All marked out, nice and regular, unlike slipping into old age with all its surprises and privileges."

Mom and I waited a moment then heard Gramps ask, "You got any more coffee over there? I'll have another cup and then let's go fishing."

While Gramps finished his coffee, I got my fishing tackle together and loaded it in his bright green truck. Old and repainted, I think I'll just assume it's his idea of a statement about the Green Movement. My sense of order insists there must be some hidden logic to that truck, but I don't know why it bothers me so much.

As we were driving down the lane Gramps asked me if I had anything new in my fishing kit. "Not really," I responded, "mostly old and reliable—some of the stuff you've given me."

"Sounds like a good combination. Is it okay with you if we go over to our favorite spot on the river?" he asked.

"Sure," I said. "I know you like that bend in the stream and that big flat rock you use for fishing and sitting. We've always done pretty well around there."

Gramps paused, apparently lost in thought for a moment

then allowed as how he spent more time fishing for ideas, maybe dreaming about wisdom, than fishing for fish on that rock these days. His little revelation caught me by surprise. I don't believe he'd ever spoken to me like that before.

I wondered where this was going and after a moment, I asked him, "Does your friend Walt still go fishing down there with you?"

"Sometimes," he said," but Walt isn't so much fun to go fishing with lately. The idea, hell, the realty, of getting old is just beating him up—making him cranky and critical of everything. Walt's got more money and stuff than most folks will ever have, but he just can't seem to be happy with anything. He's of the fervent opinion that the only value to retirement and old age is that it provides full employment for cardiologists, and a few other specialists, generalists and pill pushers he complains about endlessly.

"I try to remind him that along the way, we both chose to spend a good bit of time and a fair bit of money asking all sorts of medical professionals to work a miracle or two and get us to this age, and keep us here. It seems we ought to try and make something of this time—if for no other reason than to get some return on the investment.

"But even that crass argument doesn't move him. He thinks it was a bad investment, and that I've just become a philosophizing old coot. So, I'd rather sit out here with a fishing pole, letting the river hypnotize me by myself. Or better yet, with my grandson."

We were parked at the river by the time Gramps finished. I was certainly seeing a different side to my grandfather than I ever had before. As I let all that sink in, I remembered what Mom had asked me to do.

"On a different note," I said, "Mom was glad we could go fishing today because she wants me to find out what you would really like to have for your birthday. She told me you would probably say you didn't want anything, but she wants to get you the perfect gift, and I'm to persist."

Gramps chuckled, then said, "Your mom and I have been playing this game for longer than I can remember. I really don't need anything, and I'm not crazy about birthday celebrations, but I know for some reason they're important to her. Maybe there's a way to keep everybody happy."

He seemed to think for a moment, then said, "Why don't you go to Cabela's, or Roy's Tackle or someplace, and find some fancy piece of fishing equipment that you would like to have. Pick out something a bit more expensive than she's planning to spend—after all, it's got to be special. And make sure she sends you to buy it so you get the right one. Your mom will wrap it up all fancy before she gives it to me along with a piece of birthday cake. I'll be surprised and thank her for the perfect gift, and she'll be happy as can be. I'll use it a couple of times and then I'll give it to you. And everybody will be satisfied. How does that sound?"

I didn't think long before I said, "It sounds pretty deceptive, like we're cheating her with something really important to her. What if she figures it out—come to think of it, how can she not see through your scheme?"

Then I was really surprised when Gramps said, "I'm pretty sure she will see through the scheme. And then she'll be happier to realize we all got what we wanted and that you and I even went to extra effort to make her happy."

"That just doesn't seem logical."

"Of course not, not to a young engineering student. You're being trained to see the world as discrete parts directly and logically connected to one another in a precise manner, leading to a predicted outcome—like a clock, or a

50

motor, or a bridge. Predictably. Reliably. All the time. I was like that at one time."

Gramps went on, "From my perspective, with seven decades plus of living, one will have encountered a lot of situations where the parts, often times people, in a given situation didn't connect directly, or reliably. The relationships were more nuanced and the outcomes less certain. With old age comes the realization that we have a much larger library of experiences to draw from than anyone from a young age could yet have acquired. Getting to old age, many of us will have traveled down lots of roads, and quite a few of those won't have been paved, to paraphrase Will Rogers. But, good roads or bad, it all adds up to acquired knowledge about the way things really work. Often that's illogical, unpredictable and surprising. It's a perspective that sometimes lets us function as grease for the grinding gears between generations. That mediating role is an earned privilege and a great value of old age.

"Your mom and I have played this birthday game a lot of times. The circumstances are always a little different. Some years it's a little more intense than others, and the outcomes vary as well. But it's a good-natured game and the intentions are well understood by both of us. So, Jamie, she will figure out our play. I can promise you she will be happy, and she won't be mad at you. Most likely you'll find yourself an invited participant every year from now on.

"Sadly though, I can't get my friend Walt to see any virtue in play or fishing, or anything else. It seems he just wants to be old and miserable. Watching Walt and the way he's choosing to react to getting older saddens me. I know he's entitled to live his own life anyway he wants. But he's gotten me looking for a better view of old age for myself. There are certainly plenty of older folks around. There must be some significant value to old age or you'd think human evolution would have weeded it out by now.

"I've been filling your ears and holding you up for a while," Gramps said. "Are you ready for some fishing yet?"

I wasn't sure if I was supposed to be taking notes, expecting a test later, or if Gramps was just letting off steam and frustration. I liked hearing him talk and was pleased he seemed to be treating me like an adult, even if I was still a TWEENDER. But I was ready. With my fly rod in hand I headed for the edge of the stream and asked, "Where do you suppose those big old guys are hiding this morning?"

"Your guess is probably as good as mine. What do you think about that deeper water dug out along the bend on the other side?" Gramps said.

"Well, they could be lying there in the shadows just waiting for a juicy fly to come landing on the water in front of them. I'll give it a try," I said. Then I realized Gramps wasn't carrying a rod. "Aren't you going to do any fishing today?"

"Oh, it's such a beautiful day out here. I thought I'd sit on my thinking rock, listen to the water, and watch you doing all the work. I'm no longer as skilled at landing the fly on the right spot as you are anyway. Maybe part of me will root for you. And part of me will quietly cheer for the fish. And we'll see how that works out. Have fun."

So, I started to lay out line trying to tempt one of those wise old fish to come out and play. I was enjoying myself and thought Gramps was too, in his own way. But I was pretty sure he wasn't through philosophizing yet.

The sound of the water that morning and the rustle of soft breeze in the trees really could carry your thoughts away.

The swish of the line back and forth over my head as I played the line and the stream got me almost hypnotized.

Then I heard Gramps with a soft, almost reverent voice, "You know, Jamie, the natural setting here this morning is simply mystical. I watch the constant motion of the water and listen to it bubbling along over the rocks and shallows, and I can imagine the stream taking my spirit along with the bubbling water.

"The river has form but at the same time it's formless. It just adjusts itself to the shape of the banks and bubbles over the smaller rocks. And when it encounters a bigger obstacle, like a boulder, it splits and glides smoothly along both sides, meets again on the other side, and continues along its journey, seemingly unperturbed by the adjustments it had to make. It's a beautiful metaphor for a happy life. I'd love to ride along for a while."

Listening to Gramps, I realized this was becoming a special day for the two of us, even if I was having little success getting those fish to bite. Soon Gramps was moving along with his story again, and I was thinking this trip never was about actual fishing. Rather it was something my grandfather felt he needed to do with me. For a fleeting moment an image crossed my mind of a campfire by the river with a wise old medicine man relating tribal lore to a group of young men. I guess Gramps was getting to me. We took a few moments to quietly enjoy the sense of being really close to nature, and then Gramp's voice brought me back to reality.

He said, "You know, I'm trying to come to some better understanding of life and old age for myself. I've thought a lot about what I've seen and all the changes in my own life span. And I've found a whole lot of stuff that's been written about getting old and perhaps even enjoying the experience. Some of it even makes sense.

"One idea that keeps coming up is how most of us in our modern world have lost touch with nature and the natural rhythms of all life. There's birth, growth, and ultimately death to everything. It's natural, and each is a necessary part of a whole life."

I was not sure why I was hearing this now, so I asked: "Is there some particular lesson you expect me to learn this morning?"

"No ... I guess there isn't any particular lesson," Gramps said. "I just wanted to have a grandpa - grandson talk with you. I glad you've grown up around a farm and the river. I think it will give you an appreciation for wonder in the world, and respect for the natural order of things that most folks you'll meet will never understand. I want to be sure you understand that yourself.

"Somehow it seemed important for me to offer some of my perspective; like it's part of this old man's job to pass on a bit of culture's story. But, when I started thinking about talking with you some weeks ago, I didn't realize how much it would become mostly learning about myself."

Gramps had my attention now. The line from my fly rod was just drifting down the river, pretty much unattended. If one of those wily old fish took the bait now it would be a joke on me. But I was ready to hear what else Gramps had to say.

"Jamie, you're a fine young man, and I think the world of you. You're halfway through a bio-engineering program at the university. But you're just getting started with a challenging career. You're a smart fellow, and life has been pretty good to you so far, but I doubt it will get easier for you from here on. I expect there will be a lot of bumps in the road ahead. That's certainly been the case for most of

54

us. I hope you'll be able treat them as just bumps and not the end of the world—though some may hit pretty hard. Life will become less structured in some ways and more controlling in others, once the world really gets its hands on you. There will be lots of decisions and uncertain actions to take in the future. Have confidence in yourself, and don't let the crowd sway you too much. I hope your choices will serve you well. And call if I can help."

"Wow!" All that, I thought. Then I asked Gramps, "How do I learn to make those good decisions?"

"You learn from experience," Gramps said.

Then I asked, "Where do I get that experience?"

"Boy, you bit on that bait pretty hard," Gramps said. "It's an old cliché that us aged folks finally come to really appreciate. You get that experience from making a lot of bad decisions—and learning to live with them."

"Which brings me back to my own situation." Gramps said. "I told you I spent a lot of time sitting on this old rock, and trying to sort things out for myself. I expect most old folks do that, unless they're like my friend Walt, and choose to give up and just grumble. I don't know how long I've sat here going over my life, trying to figure out how to be wise, searching for wisdom. Then a few days ago I came across a short story entitled *Wisdom and I* by Kahlil Gibran. Jamie, you probably haven't heard of Kahlil Gibran, but I expect you will eventually. Anyway, in the story he relates how the Spirit of Wisdom visits him one night to hear Kahlil complain about all the woes and doubts of his life and what awaits beyond the gulf of darkness at life's end. 'Tell me, Wisdom, what are all these things?' he implores of the spirit.

"The story continues and Wisdom speaks, 'You, Man, would see the world with the eyes of God and grasp the secrets of the hereafter by means of human thought. Such is the fruit of ignorance. … The world that moves with you is your heart, which is the world itself. And Man, whom you deem so small and ignorant, is God's messenger who has come to learn the joy of life through sorrow and gain knowledge from ignorance. … March on. Do not Tarry, and fear not the thorns or the sharp stones on Life's path.'

"Somehow," Gramps said, "that just kind of resonates. I think I've come to believe that while you may strive to act wisely, no matter how hard you try; wisdom is not something you can acquire. Wisdom just visits you once in a while. Maybe it helps to have good intentions, but just appreciate her visits when they occur."

"Geeze Gramps, I think you're pretty wise," I said.

"Well, Jamie, you're a good fellow, and I appreciate the thought; but I can't help thinking your breadth of comparison is fairly limited. I've sure done plenty of darn fool things in my life. Yet, here we are now, more or less all right with the world, at least for today.

"Sometimes people ask me if I'd make the same decisions over again, if I had a chance to repeat them," Gramps went on. "I usually tell those folks I'd probably do things the same way as before. After all, every piece is part of what made me the way I am now. And I can live with me the way I am now. I suppose there will be some more experiences that might add on some changes. But the weight of all that past stuff has largely determined the basis of me now."

Gramps explained how he'd gone back to read some of Carl Jung's work, especially Jung's views on aging. Gramps went on, "According to some of Jung's theories on aging, the primary task of old age is to integrate all the stuff that sits in your conscious awareness with all of your subconscious stuff, and complete the process of growing up and finally becoming a complete individual. In short, the idea is to look at all the good and bad, the light and dark of your life, and accept that as what you are. It's not about being judgmental. It's just understanding that all that stuff is really part of the whole you. At least, that's my rather simple grasp of his view of life and one's psyche."

By now I had reeled in my line and given up catching anything with fins and scales. My grandfather had brought me into a different part of his world than I had ever experienced before, and I was all ears. Gramps had paused for a moment as though he was preparing another idea. Then he began again.

"Jamie," he said, "I don't want you to think I'm living in despair. This introspection trail I'm going down is really pretty exhilarating for me. It was a bit dismal at first—there's so much stuff out there that suggests getting into old age is just all aches and pains and nothing worthwhile. And it's easy to find old folks who think and act that way. But there's more to it than that. If an old guy will let go of the values and ambitions of youth, which just don't fit with his current age and abilities anymore, he can be released to find value in a new old age. In turns out there are plenty of virtues to old age if one chooses to draw on experiences and act on them. It's kind of all about attitude. I found one item among Jung's writings that especially offers me a good bit of comfort. 'The privilege of a lifetime is to become who you really are.' Jung wrote among his ideas on aging well."

Then Gramps said, "The really great part is Jung's belief that the time when the world actually lets you exercise that privilege is in old age. Hurray! I've got license to be myself. I may even paint a yellow racing stripe on my green truck. Just because I want to! Jamie, I know that bright green color on my truck bothers you. Think of it as an old man's benign rebellion toward society's constraining social norms. Just accept that your Gramps can be different."

"Good grief, Gramps. You've filled my head to near bursting. Where's this all going with us? Do you have any advice for me about how I should live?"

Gramps shook his head and chuckled as he said, "It's your life. You live it anyway you want to. I'm not telling you how to make your life's choices. I'm busy enough trying to come to grips with my own life. I hope you will be well and do good. But it's all up to you. I have confidence in your ability to handle life's uncertainties. I'm sure you will have lots of roads to travel down; I can only hope your choices will serve you well."

Contemplating a rich uncertain future, I had to ask my Gramps once more: "With all your experience, can't you offer some advice about choosing wisely along all these roads you see in my future?"

Gramps got up from his sitting rock and headed for the truck as he said, "In the memorable words of Yogi, the sage of home plate: 'When you come to a fork in the road, take it!' "

Donald N. Soderberg, PhD was born on May 24, 1941 in South Bend, Indiana. His formal education included Purdue, Notre Dame, and Tulane Universities, culminating in the PhD in Management Science from Tulane. He worked in academic and business organizations, large and small, principally in the areas of Operations and Finance.

Significant stops along the way included Indianapolis, New Orleans, San Antonio, Chicago, Washington, D.C. and Bloomington, IL. In 2010 he retired from Illinois Graphics, Inc after fifteen years as COO/CEO and moved to the Ozarks. Now he feeds his curiosity and tries to re-invent himself in Northwest Arkansas where he lives with Mariellen Griffith, his wife of twenty-eight years.

Hillary Rettig

Time Travel for Amateurs

By

H.L. Rettig

"I'm a time traveler."
"What do you mean?"
*"Every night I close my eyes and when I open them
again I'm in the future."*

When I was a kid, time seemed relentlessly linear, and I
was on the butt end of that line. For some, youth isn't a
golden age, but a time of intense unhappiness and
confusion—and, also, impatience, as you cool your heels
waiting...and waiting...and waiting for things to improve.

Like a lot of unhappy kids, I acquired the habits of: (1)
looking forward (to an adulthood I hoped would be
happier), and (2) retreating into fantasy worlds, both my
own and others'. Growing up post-Sputnik, I was a huge
fan of both science and science fiction. *Star Trek, 2001: A
Space Odyssey,* and *Silent Running* gave me hope, as did
Clarke, Asimov, etc. (Even at their most dystopic, they
presaged that there would at least be a future.)

In my twenties, and well into my thirties, still thinking
linearly and also feeling a lot of pressure to maximize every
moment and not miss a single thing, I went for singular
events and peak experiences. I did a ton of travel, had some

great lovers, and did some interestingly reckless stuff that never quite crossed the line into real danger.

Fortunately, though, at some point, I became aware of the cycles. Or, as the great songwriters Alan and Marilyn Bergman put it:

Like a circle in a spiral, like a wheel within a wheel
Never ending or beginning on an ever spinning reel
As the images unwind, like the circles that you find
In the windmills of your mind!

At first, I could only see the cycles with very rapid frequencies (they reoccurred a lot) or large amplitudes (they packed an emotional punch).

Later, I got better at spotting the subtler ones. *Everything* repeated, I realized: relationships, jobs, destinations, even meals.

I resented this a bit at first—and, to be honest, it scared me. Was I getting jaded or cynical, like so many people seem to do? But my awareness of the cyclical nature of life turned out to be mostly a good thing. Novelty-seeking—especially when fueled by what we now call FOMO ("fear of missing out")—can be exhausting and not particularly illuminating. (It's a kind of addiction, really.) *Pace* Santayana: even if you *do* know your history, you can be doomed to repeat it.

What I eventually learned was that, far from being repetitious, the cycles were actually mulligans: precious second (and third, etc.) chances. And so, I stopped resenting them and started embracing them, and life got better as a result.

The older I got, the more of these precious cycles I was privileged to experience and learn from. A few years ago, all "my" professionals—doctor, dentist, etc.—started retiring, forcing me to start over again with disconcertingly younger models.

Ditto for public figures, all the way up to the former president of the United States.

And check out this beaut: when I was attending college in Ithaca, New York, in the 1970s, the big local news was about how the new Evil Suburban Mall would devastate all the quaint 'n' quirky downtown shops. Twenty years later, the ESM had indeed done its work, and the downtown looked bleak. But now, twenty years after *that*, Amazon et al. have decimated the ESM, and the quaint and quirky downtown shops once more reign.

A cycle doesn't have to be rare to pack a punch, however. At age sixty, I've lived through exactly 240 seasonal shifts, but each one continues to fill me with awe.

And even after all these decades bedtime remains the ultimate solution to a bad day. Lucky enough to never have suffered from clinical depression or a similar malady, a brief jaunt into the future was and is usually all it takes for me to "reset" to a sunnier (yup) outlook.

Now, however, the cycles are starting to run their course. It's because of the losses—of people (including, of course, nonhuman loved ones), capacities, and potentials—each one a permanent subtraction, a dark streak in the video. And of course, they add up: at first, slowly, and then with increasing speed, until the final curtain drops. Memory— poor, frail, pale, and waning—is, let's face it, a poor compensation. But in the absence of a time machine, time-tunneling cosmic wormhole, or helpful Dr. Who-type timelord, what's a poor mortal do?

Ram Dass and the mindfulness crew suggest we, "be here now." Life may resemble a malfunctioning "wild mouse" ride that ends with an abrupt smash into a wall, but it helps if, along the way, we can stay in the moment. The best science fictional treatment of this is probably "The Inner Light," the Tao-influenced episode of *Star Trek: The Next Generation* in which Captain Picard's consciousness winds up being kidnapped so that he lives an entire alternate life in his head—forty years' worth!—in just thirty minutes of "real" time. Embedded in a new reality, he *knows* he's captain of a starship, but everything and everyone around him says no—and so, after spending five years trying to recover what he's convinced is his true life, he finally gives up and accepts the life he finds himself in.

Even more poignantly, this also includes accepting the fact that the lovely world he now inhabits is rapidly dying, and everyone he loves will die with it.

And so, like all of us but only more so, Picard finds himself pinned between a past and a future shrouded in loss. He nevertheless manages to create a life for himself, primarily by living in the now. As he at one point passionately advises his daughter, "Make now always the most precious time. Now will never come again."

(Pausing for just a second just to follow his advice...)

Taking things to the next level, you might envy the squidlike "heptapod" aliens from the movie *Arrival* (based on a short story, "Story of Your Life," by Ted Chiang) whose "now" seemingly encompasses all of their past and future. So, no losses? No! You get to live with all your losses, in extreme immediacy and vividness, all the time.

No thanks.

It's interesting to note that, restored to his "real" life and timeline, Picard doesn't retire to the family vineyard to contemplate his "now" among the grapes, but keeps on trekkin'. Just because you're mindful doesn't mean you can't swashbuckle. (In fact, it probably helps.) Meanwhile,

Henry DeTamble, the "chrono-impaired" protagonist of Audrey Niffenegger's brilliant novel, *The Time-Traveler's Wife*, is just trying to get through a life in which, at any moment, he can be yanked days, weeks, years, or decades into the past or future. Still, he's got flair; and in his final missive to his wife Clare proclaims that, compared with the great love he will always have for her, "Time is nothing."

Like Picard, I do a lot of trekking—albeit on a somewhat smaller scale. (I also spend a fair amount of time resisting Borglike entities trying to assimilate me into their homogenizing totality, but that's a subject for another essay.)

And like Henry and Clare, I've always been willing to gamble and sacrifice for love. (As Billy Joel puts it, in his song "The Longest Time," "I have been a fool for lesser things.")

Living in the now is just half the battle, however: according to the mindfulness crew, you also have to get rid of your ego. Do that, and you apparently no longer have to worry about smashing into a wall, because you *become* the wall. (As Buddha said to the hot dog vendor, "Make me one with everything.") Being still mostly subsumed in ego myself, however, and unlikely to get *un*subsumed anytime soon, I'll leave this one to other, more enlightened beings to expound on.

One way or another, however, we're all destined to rejoin the universe—which, according to scientists, *isn't* likely to hit a wall, but go on expanding forever. At the same time, a vast amount of the universe's mass is—and will continue to be—in orbit around something bigger. (Fun fact: our solar system takes a quarter billion years to orbit the black hole at the Milky Way's core.) So, in the end, on at least a physical / molecular level, we all revert to a weird mix of (sorta) linear time and cycles.

So, I guess we all know where you'll be finding me—or, at least, my swashbuckling atoms—over the next few billion years.

Unless that time-tunneling cosmic wormhole thing does turn up—in which case, stay tuned for a revision of this essay.

H.L. Rettig is author of *Joyful Productivity for Undergraduates*, *The 7 Secrets of the Prolific*, and other books. Born in the Bronx, NY, she has lived in Ithaca, NY and Boston, MA, and now resides in Kalamazoo, MI, with her partner, a physics professor. A living kidney donor (donating is another form of time-travel so check it out!), she's a lover of life, dogs, literature, social justice, and veganism. For more on Hillary and her work see www.hillaryrettig.com

I didn't like this!
too negative - re: politics
at the end

Gary Marchbank

Mind the Curves

By

Gary Marchbank

Why do numbers tend to become more important…more pervasive … as we age? In your 80's? Wow! You're living on borrowed time, old man, inwardly smiling because I am only a sprightly 74. Cholesterol count high? Wait … which one? Is it the good one or the bad one? I've got 8 grandkids; how many do you have? How many joints have you had replaced/operated on? We all thrive on numbers even if we try not to pay attention to them.

Numbers swirl all around us, all the time, every day, endlessly. Flip on the TV and numbers/data scroll across the bottom and/or top, giving us 'important' information we must pay attention to. Stock market ups and downs, football scores, polling results, scandals, et al, all compete for our attention. Go to the doctor and more data than you can possibly understand follows. First you have to remember your password for a medical portal website address that looks like a robot ate a thesaurus and a table of random numbers. Oh, and before they give you your information you must click on all sections of a picture of a monkey eating a banana. Although you successfully passed their electronic IQ test you will find interpreting your medical results is harder because of the blizzard of data points being measured. Life is way too confusing.

Worse still are the why questions … Why am I here? Am I fulfilling some purpose? Does my life have meaning?

Why are we having meatloaf again?

The older I get the more I want answers to the 'why' questions … You've got your own why questions, don't you … things that keep you up at night, things you ruminate on, things you find disturbing or unsolvable. Do you still believe your religious teachings? Will you outlive your spouse? Will the bank realize your password is a series of swear words directed at them? Why am I having such homicidal thoughts about (Name Redacted …)? We all have those nagging questions and can sometimes get stuck on one which begins to dominate your life in insidious destructive ways. Know this: It's a common malady and everybody wastes time thinking about such things. Perhaps it's more prevalent among the elderly because the approaching end of life does tend to crystallize your thinking, sometimes pushing you to address long ignored issues and problems.

So do you spend time ruminating about those questions? For some odd reason I find little interest or concern about such things because I put these questions into a context that helps ameliorate any anxiety I might otherwise have. How you ask?

It's my overarching personal philosophy and it's all about the curves in our lives. Remember the old bell-shaped curve which demonstrates the distribution of some data? The midpoint, in the center, represents the statistical 'average' for a population with a diminishing number of characteristics at each polar opposite. You can see this in everyday living thru online polls released via news programs or from your chosen websites. Some curves tend to look like a bell, albeit with different proportions, but they all tell you how the data is spread. Whether you see them or not, there are curves all around us in everything we see, touch and feel; it's ubiquitous even when we don't notice them.

Think about how many things have easy and observable opposites: up and down, left and right, black and white, fat and thin, etc. That's pretty much the way the world is…opposites with a range of gradations within it.

So what? What's that have to do with the price of tea in China? Well, in my mind, it's a lot … it really describes the way the world works, our context for living. No matter where we go or what we do we are but one tiny data point on an infinite amount of curves surrounding us. An invisible yet observable set of data is there for anyone to see if they are looking. Will looking for the curves around us help us see the world better? I think so.

The tricky part about curves is that it is easier to see the big data points and not the whole range of the data. Take, for instance, the various positions on gun control. Simply mention those words and most folks immediately jump to their pro/con position without regard to the multitude of views between being FOR or AGAINST. An incredible range of options lay between those positions which frequently get ignored because it's easier to group things into 2 easy to understand opposing viewpoints. This simplicity ignores less popular thoughts because it's easier to argue about 2 opposing views than to tease out the differences between all the choices. Furthermore, while we tend to assume that being FOR or AGAINST are the most important choices there are options at both ends of the curve that get left out completely. Some folks, while fewer in numbers, will have radically opposing positions that reflect a diversity of thought which is missing in the conversation.

Take Archie Bunker, a curmudgeonly character in the

70's sit-com, *All in The Family,* and his response to one of the first hijackings where a passenger used a gun. Archie had a contrary solution to banning guns on commercial flights; he suggested arming every passenger so if anybody started shooting, somebody else could 'take him out'... Clearly a PRO gun position but not truly reflected in the typical FOR or AGAINST polling. Even the strongest gun rights supporters probably wouldn't think handing out guns to every passenger was a good idea. Recently a candidate for President of the United States suggested 'love' and positive thinking as a solution to violence. The point is that regardless of the most frequently occurring data points on a curve, the rest of the data points are still valid viewpoints. Looking at the whole curve provides us with a broader range of options, any one of which may turn out to be better than the solutions with the most support. You can broaden your frame of reference by looking at the curves.

So, of what use is the curve in our daily lives? I think it's important because it permits us ... if we really look ... to choose among a broader more accurate reflection of the choices we all have. Take a step back and carefully look at the range of available possibilities. The most popular choices may, in fact, be the most popular because of an incomplete identification of the available choices. The first step to improve your thinking is to *find the curve.* You may have to look very hard, especially if you are used to quickly choosing. Look at the whole curve carefully; look for the end points to see the full range of possibilities. Then find yourself on the curve and re-evaluate your position.

Allow the curve to help you optimize your thinking process by considering how your characteristics match up with others. Did you get the skinny genes or need to get the fat jeans? ;-) Are you controlled by them or can you make choices that alter the outcomes? Think about the curve here; remember the terrifically wide range of choices available to us. Does your DNA control you? Aside from your DNA, who are you? Are you an outlier on the curve or right smack dab in the middle?

Where did we get those attributes? Were they specifically selected for us? Think about it … Is there a 'creator' out there that rolled a set of dice with little bits of DNA (or whatever you want to call it …) for you or specifically picked out each characteristic one by one for each one of us?

It's fruitless to discuss the name of the creator … we've all got our own religions to tell us the right answer(s). From here on out I'll go with 'BIG C' to avoid a specific name and for those who think his/her/it's/they/them designations are all wrong. Hey, who's to say what the right answer is … maybe ALL our ideas about the BIG C will be right in the end in some crazy but universally understandable way. Can you imagine that? Is there a universal answer that ultimately explains that ALL religions are true? Yeah, it would be on the extreme end of the curve, but isn't it a possibility even if we don't understand how it could be true? Hmm … does sound like a good script for the Discovery Channel, doesn't it?

My belief is that we are all our own weird little deviations on every conceivable subject and, hence, find our way into this crazy system of curves which fully describes everything. That's it … there's your universe, world and population all at once! It's ALL curves! Every attribute distributed among us in a random pattern, not willy-nilly, but just randomly assigned like the size of rocks in the river. You get what you get and I get what I get. Wow … pretty aggressive (and fully unsupported …) choice for a philosophy, isn't it?

If anybody is reading this screed, I imagine you might have a question about being a random dice throw and how it fits with your vision of the BIG C and your religious teachings. Sorry about that. It might be a bit distressing to think that the Big C didn't take the time to carve you out individually, but I think it makes perfect sense for that to be the way creation was done. Assuming the BIG C believes in efficiency ... and there's no reason to think otherwise ... using an incredibly complicated algorithm to produce us rather than doing us one at a time just makes sense. Why stress over choosing a receding hairline for each and every person created when you can just toss the dice and let the chips ... hair ... fall where they may. At the end, you'll still have a big curve including all potential elements and make it home for an early dinner with BIG C Plus One or whatever he/she/they/them/it's called. Sorry...I was hoping to avoid that, but surely the BIG C has someone they see on the weekends. And yes, I have a receding hairline...

By the way, being efficient doesn't make everything easy... The Big C still had to decide where to end every curve, what sort of distribution pattern to use and to guess which 'big' choices would get the most *Likes*. And ... getting the *Likes* sorted out was a lot more difficult before Facebook was invented. Anyway, my philosophy is that our lives, our universe and everything we see and feel were created randomly, and if we really look around, we can see where we appear on the curve and use that knowledge to make wiser choices.

So why ... pray tell ... does this knowledge allow me to not worry and have fewer questions and concerns about things? The simple answer is how the BIG C did it. My sense is that the BIG C is an intelligent being and just used a relatively simple technique in creating us and our universe. Yep, just toss those dice to get a population (or a universe, too ...) of widely variable characteristics not in a sloppy way, just a practical solution to the ever present choices in your latest Universe Creating course at the university. Think about how long it would take ... even for the BIG C ... to make all of us one by one when you're going to wind up at the end with the same thing, data spread on a curve. Carefully and individually chosen selections would simply array themselves on the curve in patterns and, for want of a better word, you still just get what you get. Pitching the dice algorithmically would result in similar results and is less stress on the elbow joint.

So ... if the BIG C simply let loose the cosmic dice giving everything and everybody in the world a spin then I think we should just 'go with it'... I, not for any good reason I can think of, got a really positive toss when I wound up white, male and born in the USA. (If limited to 3 descriptive characteristics, can you think of 3 better ones describing what the winning lottery ticket looks like? I think not. If you're cocky enough to create a better description, I simply ask you to write your OWN chapter and stay out of mine!)

Each of those characteristics seems to be at the top of most any category for the positive side of the curve. I'm retired and am reasonably well off but not what you'd consider 'rich'. In nearly uncountable ways, being born to the majority group (white) in North America, and being of the male gender was really helpful to me even when I didn't even know that it was. It's virtually impossible for me to arrive at a complete understanding of how many breaks I got because I am white, male and born in the USA. I won't bother to list the ways; it's pretty obvious and overwhelming when you really think about it … Hint: Google it!

So, my overarching philosophy is that we mostly live in a random world and seeing the curves around us helps to figure out where we are and where we can/should go. Is my destiny fixed and unchangeable? Of course not, but I was 'given' certain attributes and tendencies and, absent activity on my part to change their trajectory, they will tend to push me and my behavior in those ways. I think observing the curve gives you a perspective on the range of possibilities to help you sort out things. Am I going to be a multi-millionaire with a home in the Hamptons? Well, I'm 74 and I don't think that's in the cards for me. I don't know where I'll wind up; but I know I've had a good life so far, and I'm not going out without enjoying what I can. Yeah, I've had my share of sorrows along the way; but I've made it this far, so I'll just keep plugging along, but I won't worry.

So why don't I worry about my path in the future? Well, what's the point? Really, what's the point of doing so? Worrying ain't going to change a thing and time spent doing that limits how many episodes of *Everybody Loves Raymond* I can watch. I'd rather laugh aloud than moodily frown about my lack of a bigger bank account, a better looking face or whatever else I could stew about!

So what about asking the BIG C for a do over or a second chance at winning the lottery? Here's my experience with talking to the BIG C… great listener but mostly the strong silent type … terrific as a sounding board but doesn't work like a Ouija board where you can push the pointer toward *Yes* when nobody's looking. Every time I've requested fewer pounds of flab on my body a voice in my head says 'cut carbs' but that's usually my wife rather than a response to prayer! Maybe the BIG C does miracles from time to time but, in my own life, I've not seen any burning bushes except for that time we almost caught the woods on fire. (Being completely honest, I did experience one miracle in my life, but that's a long story and you sort of had to be there to appreciate it. Maybe that'll be discussed in a different book ... If not, you'll have to trust me; it was way cool!)

Anyway, worrying just ain't worth the time in my humble opinion. Try it at your peril and don't expect any miracles. So ... to me, it's ALL a big crap shoot, all of it and you've just got to use what you've got to get where you want to be.

My take on aging is that you can't stop it, you can't go backwards and change your decisions, and you are foolish if you waste a lot of time worrying about it. What you can do is to make the most of what you've got, think long term when you can and find the most optimal path to getting what you think you want. Short of that, acceptance and persistence is about all you've got left. OK, maybe you can get an injection or two, do a slice and dice on your belly fat and feel better about yourself but, in the end, it's still just you and your problems when you close your eyes at night. Someday you'll close your eyes one final time and, hopefully, feel like you've lived a good life and deserve to rest for a while...

So my words of wisdom about aging are really simple... Observe the invisible curves all around us to better understand how you and the world fit together. Modify your chosen path to the extent you can with the tools you have and throw the worry stick into the nearest trashcan. I must leave you, however, with one last thought about you and the world.

The Great Societal Intrusion and Time Suck

Whether old or young, our collective time on earth is sometimes beset with unexpected intrusions, disruptive events which consume societal time and attention. Most are small and of short duration, maybe a day, a couple of weeks or months. Others linger on indefinitely and become endless but obligatory in the news cycle ... wars (religious, territorial, insurgencies et al), natural disasters, changing climate, pollution, and other catastrophic events.

Normally, political machinations and shenanigans grab our attention and divert us from our everyday life but end reasonably quickly, their shelf life constrained by election cycles and dwindling public attention. And then there is Donald Trump...

The day the Trumpster slowly came down the escalator marked a highly significant change in the way one politician came to dominate our lives. I won't attempt any description of him whether positive or gleeful or gloomy beyond belief; many others have already done this. His presence on the world stage has simply sucked a lot of the air out of the room/world and moved him and his minions into the forefront of our minds whether we want that or not. The Donald pops to the front of the news queue so much that we would need another 24-hour news cycle just to cover him adequately.

I feel both drained and cheated, sad and worn out ... mentally broadsided by his ubiquitous presence ... and wishing I had every second of time back I found myself thinking about him. Trying to quantify my loss is extraordinarily difficult, his impact so wide spread and pervasive. I used to enjoy keeping up with the news of the world but now not so much. It's too sad to look at but hard to look away. Either way, I've squandered too much valuable time on him. I think many others feel the same way but are caught between trying to 'make a difference' and not give up. Historians will look back on this era with amazement that this guy once consumed the world's attention and will wonder why.

So why is this important to those of us in our 'golden years'? It's all about the curve, isn't it? The older you are the less time you have on this earth. Right? Then, how do you want to spend your remaining time? Listening to endless and mostly unproductive 'debate' about the Trumpster's behavior? Isn't that a huge waste of time? So don't do that. At a minimum, resolve to be more careful about your use of time.

On the other hand, the Trumpster is an extreme outlier which shows that in the game of life, like horse racing, long shots do make it into the money. You may be nearing the end of your curve, but you're still alive now so there is still hope. Maybe you're facing adversity, worries and temptations, and find little reason to hope. Remember this: there is always some hope on the curve; maybe the Golden Ticket is just around the corner. Be realistic, but know that long shots still win!

So, if you are likewise involuntarily consumed by the Trumpster, here's my unsolicited advice:

Pro-Trump Readers:
Enjoy the ride while you can; but remember, this too shall pass. Every carnival needs a barker but eventually the party will be over and others will clean up and empty the trash. The time will come when the mention of his name will bring a collective cry of relief to the world.

Anti-Trump Readers:
Avoid the primate exhibit; you will be 'dunged' if you get

too close. Tomorrow may be a brighter day; plan and work for it.

Gary Marchbank is a retired social worker who spent most of his career working in the low income and child welfare programs at the local, state and federal level. Retirees frequently say they miss the people but not the work; Gary liked them both. He received an undergraduate degree in Sociology from Missouri State and a Master's Degree in Social Work from the University of Missouri. In retirement he is active in church and civic groups, and is on the Advisory Board of the local Food Pantry. Mr. Marchbank loves to sing and, although he's not very good at it, has been singing tenor in church choirs since high school. He always sits as far away from the microphones as possible and strains to reach anything above a high E. Mr. Marchbank proposed to his beautiful wife, Lou, a week after they met in college and married less than a year later. They have been married for over 50 years and still speak to each other fondly. She is the best thing that ever happened to him. They have four wonderful children, all of whom married well, and have eight grandchildren. The grandkids are interesting and fun to be with and there's not a clunker in the bunch. The Marchbanks live outside a small town in Missouri with a dog and 11 chickens.

Jim Long

When Gardens Die

By

Jim Long

A television interviewer asked Tasha Tudor, the famed American writer and children's book illustrator, what she thought would happen to her remarkable garden in Marlboro, Vermont when she was gone. "Oh, it'll be gone in six months after I'm dead," she said matter of factly. "Weeds will take over; no one will remember where each plant came up each season. It's just a garden as long as I'm the gardener."

I look at my own garden and wonder whether that's enough for me. Does it really matter that after I'm gone no one will remember in which bed the lemon balm grew, or whether the shave grass soon escapes its container and runs unchecked all over the place? I recently made out a will, something many people don't seem to take care of until later in life. I put it off for years, but when finished, it no longer seemed the morbid act I had imagined it to be when I was younger. That decision to write my will was brought on by a decision I had made to fulfill a lifetime's desire of visiting West Papua, New Guinea, to one of the most remote, stone-age cultures left anywhere on earth. Writing my will spurred me to think again about my garden's longevity and what would eventually happen to this heavenly spot.

I imagine that all gardeners wonder what will happen when they leave their gardens. The relationship between a gardener and his or her plants is a very intimate, personal one, more like a relationship with a pet or a close friend. After all, for most of us, the garden is our personal paradise on earth, our most relaxing spot and the place where we can feel most in control of the world around us. Like my favorite saying goes, "I live in the garden; I only go to the house to sleep."

Before I obtained this farm, Dale and Stella White had gardened here for most of their lifetimes. Both had grown up within walking distance of where they chose to settle. They had bought the property as newlyweds from a relative, built a simple house, and grew their own produce for over half a century, canning, drying and preserving all they could for their survival. They surely were filled with hope and excitement at the process of creating a life for themselves on this amazing piece of land. They must have felt it was their own personal paradise, as well. How many aching backs from hoeing did they have, how many pounds of home-grown sausage did they season with their garden's sage and peppers, and how many times did they look out at their garden and admire it in the moonlight, as I do mine, year in and year out?

I was well acquainted with Dale and Stella. After I acquired the property four decades ago, the Whites moved a couple of miles down the road, moved to a trailer house and made themselves a new garden. In their retirement they needed less garden but spoke often of how they missed their earlier spot. I visited them off and on for years until they died. We often talked about what they grew and how they lived here fifty years ago and how much they loved this place.

During the 1940s and 1950s Dale and Stella grew both goldenseal *(Hydrastis canadensis)*, which they knew as "yellowroot," and ginseng *(Panax ginseng)* as cash crops to sell to traveling root buyers who came through the area in the fall. Table Rock Lake now covers the wooded area along Long Creek where they once harvested the roots of these two important medicinal herbs. Today, pastureland and wooded hillsides rise above the lakeshore above the creek where they harvested the herbs. Many years ago, I planted some goldenseal in my own garden, and I think of Dale and Stella whenever I see its tiny white blossoms and crinkly olive-green leaves in springtime and watch as the red seed clusters form in mid-season.

My goldenseal thrives in moist, fertile soil, planted in a spot near a grapevine-covered arbor where it receives morning sun but fully shaded during the rest of the day. Growing next to it are other native herbs including ginseng, pinkroot *(Spigelia marilandica)*, violets *(Viola* spp.) and native sweet cicely *(Myrrhis odorata)*. Coltsfoot *(Tussilago farfara)*, wild ginger *(Asarum canadense)* and bloodroot *(Sanguinaria canadensis)* also grow nearby as they might do in a natural setting. Each year I renew the mulch for the herb beds with pine needles; but otherwise, I don't disturb the little plantings, leaving them to spread and reseed in their own growth cycles.

Occasionally in early spring when I am tilling the soil, I find an arrowhead or sometimes a flint hoe-shaped tool. I easily imagine earlier Native peoples here, growing their own food in this garden spot. Countless generations of Natives lived on this land, fishing the streams, hunting in the woods and growing beans, squash, corn and related crops. A metate I found nearby attests to the grinding of corn and grains and seeds in this spot. To those earlier people, and to Dale and Stella, I have no doubt this was their own paradise, a place of not only sustenance but pride, renewed through many generations of people.

There is no doubt that countless families have gardened in "my spot." Many struggled, as I have, but have also basked in the beauty of growing their food, of watching the cycles of the seasons as they come and go and rising to the challenges of weather, insects and wildlife.

Those who went before me are all gone now; and Dale and Stella's last garden where they lived most recently has been bulldozed for a new landowner's home, yet I can't help but feel a bit of them survives in my own garden in the plants they nurtured and grew. The heritage of the native peoples who toiled here is honored by the tools they left. Maybe the best legacy for me to leave for some future gardener is a bounty of wild and naturalized plants scattered among the winding stone walls and pathways I've built, and maybe a few lost tools, as well. I can only hope that whoever lives here in the future will find as much pleasure as I have had in tending the soil and growing something new and wonderful each year that feeds both body and my soul.

Jim Long is a professional gardener and author of more than two dozen books on herbs, gardening and historical subjects. He has written for many national and regional gardening publications including *The American Gardener, Edible Austin* and *The Heirloom Gardener,* with 2 decades of columns for *The Herb Companion, Missouri Gardening* and a syndicated newspaper column that ran for 20 years. Jim has appeared on numerous HGTV® and Discovery Channel® programs, the P. Allen Smith Gardens Show®

and is a frequent speaker at conferences, festivals and garden shows nationwide. His gardens have been featured in numerous national publications including *Southern Living* (twice), *Gourmet, Better Homes and Gardens, Garden, Deck and Landscap*e, and many more. His reputation for gardening brought him an invitation from Workman Publishing in New York, to provide fresh herbs and help prepare a special Presidential brunch for then President and First Lady, Bill and Hillary Clinton in Washington, D.C. in 1992.Insatiable curiosity and a desire to share has taken Jim around the world to places as diverse as the remote jungles of West Papua, New Guinea and the crowded markets of India. He studied cooking in Thailand and lectured at the first International Slow Food Conference in Turin, Italy alongside such notables as Michael Pollan and Alice Waters. Jim continues his passion for plants, inspiring gardeners with his many books, columns, articles and blogs. His gardens can be toured from his website LongCreekHerbs.com

Ernest Leonard

Ally on My Shoulder

By

Ernest Leonard

Death

Every morning I hear the drums waking the monks in the *wat* (Buddhist temple) next to our home. Soon after, our dogs and I go for an amble around the back of the wat and on the way, we stroll past the crematory (*passha* in Lao) a hundred or so meters beyond to the edge of Tat Luang Marsh. Late afternoons Bobo and Puppy demand the same excursion. The *passha* is an open area of about three acres with a covered gathering structure on one side. Here the families, friends and attending monks view three concrete pyre platforms. They are topped with steel enclosures that contain the large timbers used to fuel the burning of the departed in elaborate, gold trimmed paper and wood coffins with soaring canopies. Most often, on our morning strolls families and workers are there setting out plastic chairs, portable awnings and fuel timber for one or more ceremonies to send off some souls. In the afternoons we see the embers dying and relatives waiting for the ashes to cool so they can take the bones for an ossuary and perhaps, if they have the money, a stupa to contain them. And again, I am reminded.

As I walk by, I am reminded of Don Juan the Mexican Indian brujo. Don Juan was the shaman teacher creation of the 60's new age writer Carlos Castaneda. I remember little of what I read in Castaneda's books except Don Juan's metaphorical description of death as an ally who sits on one's left shoulder. The death ally is there to remind us all of the finite nature our existence and the urgency to take the gift of life on a moral path.

As we pass the *passha* my ally whispers in my left ear, "*I am here.*" My ally reminds me that at seventy-seven years I am exceedingly lucky to be alive, ambulatory and only moderately cognitively challenged. (Well, my family might dispute the last part.) My ally reminds me of joys and sorrows that I have experienced and created with my life. And I am reminded that there are still things to do with whatever is left.

Gifts

Age has somewhat tempered the grasping, almost desperate egoism of my soul and challenged me to accept some of what Henri Nouwen describes as the discipline of gratitude. Though I find myself to be a rather poor servant to the discipline, life continues to deliver encounters with people and events that fill me with gratitude. Family, teachers, colleagues and friends; with few exceptions, all have been, and continue to be, uncommonly generous and forbearing with me throughout my entire life. At the same time there is the realization of the need to take ownership of how I became the person I am. So, there is a great desire to express the gratitude I feel for gifts received, regrets for transgressions committed and ingratitude displayed. Oh, so many!

One unexpected gift of my old age and living in this alien culture is acceptance. I am unsure which is most influential, my age or the culture, but about eight years ago I realized I was no longer pursuing more income, more excitement, competitive advantage and needing to be constantly active.

One wonderful influence has been my wife Kek. Over the last ten years of our relationship she has constantly reminded me to *"pak pone!"* (relax). Two years ago, Kek was assisted by a Thai cardiologist who prescribed a double bypass to clean up some of the mess in my cardiovascular system. As with most other heart patients my condition was due to a decidedly immoderate sixty years of stress, consuming alcohol, tobacco and indiscriminate eating. *Pak pone* has become a true guiltless pleasure.

Late in life I left California to live in Laos, a land of Theravada Buddhism. The perceptions and treatment of the older folks in this culture are at times charming, at times frustrating and quite different from American expressions. Ageism in Laos takes other forms. Here, older persons are respected and coddled but expectations are low. When elders are active and engaged, younger Lao express wonder and exclaim how *"strong"* the old one is. And since, in this country, civil society is severely restricted there aren't many outlets for elders with energy and ideas. They usually live with their children, help with household chores, watch TV and when they can, sit around and gossip with neighbors.

What, to me, is interesting about living in this radically different culture is how little the host influences the core psyche of the guest and how little influence the guest has with the host. But the guest (regardless of age) had better come to terms with and accommodate the differences. I am the elder of my family in Laos but my opinions on matters of culture have little sway and often elicit resentment. For example, before our daughter-in-law was to give birth, I questioned the Lao tradition of *yu kam*; where for two weeks, post-partum mothers will lay on a bamboo bed over sheet pans with burning charcoal on the floor. The heat is (maybe the fumes as well) believed to restore energy and close the vaginal opening of the new mother. When seeing *yu kam* in the past I have wondered how, given the toxic nature of burning charcoal fumes, it could be a beneficial practice for mother and child. I recently expressed my concern and cautions to my wife. They were met with determined truculence. Culture is so profoundly ingrained in each of us. As I write this Mother Jai is reclining on the bamboo bed with Baby Peyton (Yes, think Colts and Broncos!) and beneath, the charcoal is smoldering.

Whys

While I don't have much interest in reliving my past, my soul seems to be asking questions, mostly "why" questions. Why the multiple marriages? Why the crazy risk-taking as a youngster? Why the incessant restlessness? And, why, since my mid-sixties, have I come to feel more settled? Why didn't this peace come before? The only answer I can conjure is; *old age*. It seems to me that, since puberty, I lived with a surfeit of testosterone and, for whatever reasons, deficits of self-awareness and self-confidence. Maybe the in-vogue term, "ownership" has something to do with it. Could it be that as one ages the hormones align with the reality of one's life, and as the scales fall, we get a real look in the mirror.

Looking Around

We pre-baby boomers and baby-boomers came into the world at a wonderful time in America and Western Europe. We have had the privilege of enjoying massive economic growth and opportunity. We have participated in developing global communication, urbanization and expanding awareness and grudging codification of civil rights and environmental preservation. Most of us who graduated from college in the 1960s had no debt and jobs were there for just about any who wanted one. Craftsmanship was still respected and generally rewarded. But then we introduced credit cards and other debt instruments that opened the door for massive wealth transfers from the growing number of working folks who wanted the *good life now* to those who controlled the financial system. At the same time, working folks found themselves assuming more of the risk in the globalized economy through the loss of employment retirement programs, health benefits and often the elemental protections of being an "employee." I simply marvel at the gifts those times gave us and how little we appreciated them and how, as a society, we have neglected to fully leverage them for global stability, social justice and environmental preservation.

In my reading of history, it seems old folks have always had the reputation of believing their world is on the precipice of disintegration. Our generation has good reason for these sentiments. On this basis alone I hope to live another ten years. Can the human species address looming catastrophes of global heating, plastic pollution, internet connectivity, nuclear proliferation, maldistribution of resources and Trumpism? My bet, unfortunately, is no, and I believe the next ten years are likely to be decisive. Perhaps there is a cruel perversity in my soul, but I do want to be around to see how things play out.

Relationships

Our existence is an ephemeral event. Much as we try to carve our place in history or even the memories of our contemporaries, we have to accept that, ultimately, we pass into the void that consumes all. When my father died at eighty-six my mother asked me to take the obituary she had written to the local newspaper. I went to their office and told the receptionist I had Jim Leonard's obituary for them to publish. She said, "Who?" There were several others in the office and none of them had heard of the man who grew up there, had served as a printers' devil and written for the paper and was life-long friends with the former publisher who pre-deceased him by fifteen or so years. He was born in a mining camp fifteen miles from the small northern Arizona town and spent most of his life growing up, teaching, being a school principal and serving the community. On his retirement from the school district he was grandly feted by the community. After he died my mother said she could think of only a very few people in town that would remember them.

I have a son, Norman, who from a very early age exhibited an inviolate sense of self and integrity. He has created a life of personal and professional success for himself that is gratifying to any parent and welcomed by his community, friends and colleagues. It was fascinating to watch him grow and realize that he seems to have a preternatural internal compass that has guided him through tough times. His intelligence and compass have also given him the good sense to use opportunities at opportune times to build a successful career, solid marriage and worthwhile life. Thank heavens some genes can skip a generation.

Paradoxically, it seems that for most of us those family, friends and community ties become more precious after retirement and into old age. It is easy to imagine why older folks who live alone and too long and have few or no friends often have it pretty tough. Even when relationships hit rough spots, underneath it all is the realization that it is the *existence* of the relationship that is the real value. Living eight thousand miles from my roots and in a different culture, I find repairing the inevitable fraying and filling the holes that occur in close relationships has become a priority. Not Easy, but a priority.

My Old Body

"Age is just a number!" What crap! Through the years, I have usually maintained my vehicles quite well and driven them until they are ready to fall apart. They always looked good and ran well but the cost of keeping them on the road after ten or so years of hard driving would become prohibitive. Oh, had I treated my body so well! Only now, do I perform the same level of maintenance on my health that I did on my vehicles throughout their entire time in my possession. Fortunately, in this part of the world good medical care isn't yet too cost prohibitive! Now, no way can I look in the mirror and proclaim the vacuous idea that "seventy-seven is the new fifty-seven". My seventy-seven looks and feels seventy-seven. Muscle loss, thin skin (literally, figuratively, not so much), wrinkles, diminished libido, not-to-reliable memory and aches and pains; I have the whole package. However, emotional intensity and sensitivity seems to be on the upswing. While the lows and anger are less intense, the happiness and joy are more profound. Sometimes my expressions of emotion are met with opprobrium by family and Lao acquaintances. Old Folks aren't supposed to act that way!

Over the years here in Laos I have the good fortune to have developed a circle of good and interesting friends from around the globe. Most of them are in their sixties and seventies; and since there isn't much else to do; they are still engaged in some sort of enterprise. Too often though, we catch ourselves comparing maladies and sharing various methods of dealing with them. When these topics come up, I think, *"Oh dammit, here we are again, talking about old peoples' stuff!"* Like tripping over the cat, it must be another hazard of old age. But then I consider that we are probably sharing pretty useful information and experience given we live in a country with abysmal health care and can only access good care by going to neighboring Thailand or some other country. Even so, the conversations seem to elicit the same feelings of boredom and a bit of despair in each of us.

Throughout my life, I have experienced episodes of pain sensations in my body that would send me into worries of *"Oh, my god, is this the cancer I am supposed to earn from smoking?"* or similar thinking, depending on the nature of the discomfort and where it is in my body. When the pain left or I had forgotten about it my anxiety would disappear until the next time. Doctors call it "idiopathic," (cause, unknown) pain. (One of my wives claimed it was because I *am* an *idio*!) While I have never researched this phenomena it occurs to me that it is likely that many, if not most people experience the same thing; they just don't dwell on it as I did. But, to me, in the context of this topic, ageing, I realize that, while the pains still occur; lately, I don't give a damn! And there are newer pains of *known* sources, and I don't much give a damn about them either. Thanks to occasional Tylenol or cannabis!

Looking into the Sunset

That's my story, and I'm stickin' to it. I can climb about two flights of stairs before taking a breather. But at seventy-seven I refuse to be wuss-shamed by my brother-in-law who, recently, in celebration of his eightieth birthday, hiked to the bottom of the Grand Canyon and back to the parking lot in one day.

When Puppy, Bobo and I walk to the marsh in the evenings we are often treated to gorgeous sunsets with the sun setting behind the clouds and buildings across the emerald paddy fields, trees and water. Because we have passed the *passha* and my ally always seems to accompany us, I linger and see.

Ernest Leonard was born early in 1942 in Glendale, California where his father was helping build P38 fighter planes at Lockheed Aircraft. After the war the family returned to Arizona where Ernest grew up and graduated from Northern Arizona University. After NAU he earned a PhD from Claremont Graduate School and University Center in 1973. He taught government and public finance at Long Beach State University for three years. He then started and ran a commercial construction business for six years, specializing in waterproof coatings. He returned to academia for several years to work a liaison for CSUC Academic Consortium. Ernie also served in a U.S. Fish and Wildlife think tank for preserving and restoring fish and migrating bird habitat in California's Central Valley. In 1999 he began working for Opening Doors, Inc., a non-profit agency serving refugees in the Sacramento area. He concluded his service as Vice President and director of the Community Development Financial Institution for ODI. In 2007 Ernie retired from ODI and went to Laos to help develop a health services agency. On arrival he was enchanted with the country. After eight months working in

Laos the enchantment wore off but by that time it was home and he decided to stay.

not my taste

Don Lehnhoff

Aging, Religion and the Meaning of Life

By

Don Lehnhoff

I intend to live forever. So far ... So good.
—Steven Wright

The available evidence—empirical, theoretical and anecdotal—shows pretty clearly that people embrace religious faith to a greater extent in the late stage of life. The reasons why are many, but a hedge against the prospect of eternal damnation, no matter how remote, is certainly in the mix. Depending on the degree of one's fear and anxiety about death and the unknown, it can also be a balm for the troubled mind. For a wealth of authoritative information on this subject, complete with charts and graphs, I refer you to a June 13, 2018 report from the Pew Research Center titled, "The Age Gap in Religion Around the World.[i]"

In counterpoint to the fear of impending death is the fearlessness and distraction of youth. Youngsters have no fear of death because they have no point of reference and no time for such contemplation. They simply have a whole lot more on their minds and on their plates. They know they're going to die "someday" of course, but that day is remote; not right in front of their noses like it is after a certain age.

Other than sudden death by accident or violent act, death is not an event but a process. By 70 (the "death decade" so

105

I've been told) you don't just know it's going to happen, you become acutely aware of that process and attuned to its progress. You're able to begin speculation as to just what lurking infirmity is likely to take you when the time comes. As you recognize the process at work and see much more of your life behind you than ahead, you might start looking around for a way out ... or at least a way to soften the blow.

If this search reaches a point where you're grasping at straws, religion is standing by—a big familiar straw (paper please, not plastic), stuck right in the middle of the cherry phosphate of life. The buildings and the institutions housing religion are very familiar and right there on the street corners you pass every day. Even the non-religious, non-practicing non-believer has likely had some brush with organized religion at some time in their life, so it's not a total leap into the unknown. There's a familiarity, so if your prior brush was with Catholicism you already know how to dip in the holy water and cross yourself, with Islam you know when and how to kneel and in what direction, with Puritanism you know how to ignore fun, etc.

"Even if you're not religious, live it like you're Christ."
—Mac Lethal, Speed Rapper

As of the date of this publication I am a freshly-minted 73-year-old. That puts me squarely in the crosshairs of this late life "come-to-Jesus (or whomever)" moment. For better or worse (yet to be determined) I embraced no particular spiritual conviction or specific religious practice throughout my life. When I was very young, I asked my Mother who Jesus was, and she told me he was the best person who ever lived. She added that to follow his example would be the best way to live life. I'm no different than any other boy who wants to please his mother, so I latched onto this idea.

When required to attend Sunday School I read and listened to all the Bible stories, paying particular attention to how Jesus handled himself, and that became my model. To be clear, never at any time did I aspire to 'Holiness' or think I would be a 'Holy Man' (Jim Jones and David Koresh be damned), or in any way think I was participating in religious practice. I was just following the example of a man my mother considered to be a really good guy, like you would follow your father's example, or that of an influential football coach, etc. Jesus as mentor. Another lesson from my Mother was that while I was a great kid, I was no better than anyone else. With these two themes in hand I set out to prove her right and make her proud.

[Lesson: Be careful what you tell your kid's ... they might be listening.]

While I'm sure these insights into life imparted by my wonderful Mother had some unintended consequences, seven decades of practice have made me eternally grateful for her wisdom. I'm not afraid to die, having given life my best shot. I have none of the debilitating residue of guilt imparted by the attitudes and teachings of some parents and institutions. I don't harbor regret for not having done more in life, not having made more money, or not having 'measured up' in some way. I have tried to be an honest person who treated others with respect, understanding that their dreams were just as important and valuable as my own. Thanks, Mom.

Admittedly, all of this was easier to pursue for me than some, given my random privilege as a middleclass white boy, growing up in the latter half of 20th century America. I'm also aware of the high degree of good luck required in achieving peace of mind. Be that as it may, I did my best and here I am.

Yes, here I am ... both feet in the 'death decade', devoid of personal religious faith, and with the same basic human instincts and needs as everybody else. Although I've lived my life with no specific religious or spiritual affiliation, I certainly feel a spiritual connection to life itself and all the unfathomable wonder that this existence represents. I just don't believe in magic. So ...?

What *do* I believe in? If I'm spiritual but not religious, what do I call that? I'm not really a 'label' kinda guy, so do I even need one, or want one?

Atheist?

I'm not an atheist. They believe there is no God, and to me that claim is as arrogant as declaring with certainty that God exists.

Agnostic?

I'm not an agnostic. They believe in ... *nothing*. The obvious wonders of the world all around us defy the assumption that it comes from nowhere.

Like so much information in our 'information age' my answer came by way of the inter-googly-webs.

The "Flying Spaghetti Monster" was first described in a satirical open letter written by Bobby Henderson in 2005 to protest the Kansas State Board of Education decision to permit teaching intelligent design as an alternative to evolution in public school science classes. In the letter, Henderson demanded equal time in science classrooms for "Flying Spaghetti Monsterism" [Pastafarianism] alongside intelligent design and evolution. After Henderson published the letter on his website, the Flying Spaghetti Monster rapidly became an Internet phenomenon and a symbol of opposition to the teaching of intelligent design in public schools.

—Wikipedia[ii]

"In a traditional faith, violation of the written word makes you a sinner.

In Pastafarianism, violation of the unwritten word makes you an asshole."

—The Unorthodox Pastafarian Church: Our Lady of Occasional Certitude[iii]

The whole *Flying Spaghetti Monster* thing went 'viral' before going viral was even a thing. It sparked the imagination of people around the world, myself included, and today has evolved as a way for people to have a shared 'religious' conviction and connection with others around 'non-God' things — things other than dogma, commandments, liturgy, magical thinking and such — things that are meaningful in their lives. This irreligious religiosity tends to center around temporal matters of existence—evolution and the human condition—and at its root of origin a strong opposition to wedging religious thinking as scientific theory into secular civic life.

Pastafarianism, like Christianity and other mainstream religions, is based on a foundation not of evidence, but of community. The Pastafarian church was 'built', and its legitimacy established, by people tired of being disenfranchised for thinking for themselves. The same thing drove the Pilgrims to colonize the New World. That Pastafarians don't 'literally' believe their own superstitions, or the 'real' existence of their own God, is evidence that they are, indeed, thinking.

109

Pastafarians believe in a scripture that need not be believed, or even written down for that matter. Like many Christians who themselves don't take some of the crazy stuff in their own Bible literally, so it is with Pastafarians. The Church of the Flying Spaghetti Monster[iv] myths and traditions include pasta, midgets, pirates, midget pirates, and beer. Why not?

Turning normative concepts on their ear (think G.K. Chesterton) is what the internet's long tail does best. Rather than a strong leader crafting and promoting a revolutionary concept into wider recognition and acceptance, the spread of Pastafarianism has pulled its creator, Bobby Henderson, along with it, as the idea has evolved and mutated like a runaway Andromeda's Train. Its acolytes have given it definition rather than fealty. Initially described by observers as a parody religion, it is now more often described as a social movement—a worldwide social movement. It has also been described by people professing 'true' religious faith as an atheist club, which it definitely is not; and called a sacrilege which, by definition, it certainly is. But like any religion, Pastafarianism has its own ideas about what is sacred: reality-based thinking and living, freedom from mythical influences in the organization and governance of society, and adherence to basic concepts of human dignity.

> *"For me, it is far better to grasp the Universe as it really is than to persist in delusion, however satisfying and reassuring."*
> —Carl Sagan

I have lived all of my adult life outside the bounds of organized religious practice and thinking. While showing respect to those who believe differently, as they wish, and supporting their right to do so, I have also witnessed the backward perspective of some of it that threatens harm to the tangible, non-magical world I care about. Most of all, I dislike the way such mythical thinking is allowed to intrude upon reason and decision-making in the secular realm. Pastafarianism was conceived and created in specific opposition to that.

No better (nor worse) than anyone else, I travel that same universal trajectory of life that says, given my age, I am more likely to embrace religion ... and so I have. It just took some time for the religion that resonates with me to appear. As noted at the outset, the reasons for late-life religiosity are numerous and varied, but it seems that many, if not all, revolve around one of those simple things we old folk come to recognize as fundamental, at once a driving and calming force in human existence at all ages and stages of life — hope.

Hope. People born into unfortunate circumstance latch onto it at the earliest possible moment. They must, for the alternative is despair and defeat. People born to privilege may see it differently but they see it, and embrace it. It's what gets you out of bed in the morning, motivates you in the monumental effort often required to face life, and makes each year's start of baseball spring training a moment of limitless possibility.

I'm not afraid to die, so I have no hope of avoiding it. I don't hope to go to heaven nor avoid hell, because I'm reasonably confident they don't exist (I could be wrong) — although I don't feel I'd qualify for either destination regardless. My hope is not unique. It's that simple, fundamental hope shared by many, many people. As it approaches its inevitable end, it's the hope that my life had value. Some call this their "legacy" and while that word doesn't resonate with me personally, at least part of its definition applies.

My legacy would not be one of monetary value, edifice or inheritance. I just hope I've lived in a way, using my 1/7billionth piece of the existential pie, to help nudge the flow of existence in the direction of truth and light and good will.

In the classic depiction of the search for truth it is the young person who climbs the mountain to ask the Guru the eternal question: "What is the meaning of life"? The Guru is always an old guy—could be an old gal, but there's usually a beard involved as part of the look, so.... Of course, I'm no Guru. The Guru is a Holy Man whose lifelong fasting / meditating / studying have led him to enlightenment, but enlightened as he may be, that is not the source of his knowledge on this particular issue. He knows the answer, not because he's a Guru, but because he's old. Now I'm an old guy myself, and by virtue of that fact I know the answer too.

The meaning of life is 'the future'. It is the next generation, the next evolved version of ourselves, and it's driven by the universal imperative of all living things: continuation of the species. If you want meaning in your life, live it in the present but in favor of the future. Remember the past, learn from it, leave it behind.

I know this because I'm old, and have invested all I am into this one single personal thread of existence. Regardless of how much life lies ahead, it won't come close to the vast majority that lies behind me, available for scrutiny and analysis but not one molecule of reconfiguration.

I'm going to die, that is certain (you too), and I rejoice in this knowledge for it means that I am one with every living thing that has ever existed. Death means I have lived, and I only hope that my presence in life was, on balance, a positive thing.

"When I do good, I feel good. When I do bad, I feel bad.
That's my religion."
—Abraham Lincoln

Donald Lehnhoff is a writer, musician, marketing weasel, family man and devout Pastafarian living in Minneapolis, Minnesota. He was born and raised in Baltimore, Maryland where he was exposed to the Methodist church at an early age. His work life has included delivering dry cleaning, flowers, and major appliances, trimming and harvesting Christmas trees, managing commercial & residential real estate, and selling tchotchke to hundreds of businesses, institutions and organizations. He served 2 years in the U.S. Army at Ft. Bragg, North Carolina, brandishing nothing more lethal than a trombone.

Larry Laverentz

The Paths and Footprints that Lead to Understanding

By

Larry Laverentz

"Before you go up the hill ask someone who has just come down."
~ Chinese Proverb

I do not give much thought to or worry about dying. Of course, I am aware that the shadows are lengthening but feel that I am good for at least a few more years. I like the question, "How old would you be if you did not know how old you are?" At age 81 I am in reasonably good physical and mental health, due in part to the fact I have paid attention to maintaining these over the past 30 or so years. I expect to continue to give priority to the thoughts and actions that will contribute to my longevity. The latter include actions related to diet, exercise, maintaining a reasonable weight and adhering to the prescriptions and advice of doctors. My thoughts should include feelings of gratitude and empathy, allow for humor, taking life but not myself too seriously, retaining a sense of purpose, and having a measure of tolerance and adaptability to new ways of thinking and doing things. I admit to bowing to my pride in wanting to be viewed as being younger than my 81 years.

They would gather at McFarland's in the middle of the afternoons or maybe on a rainy morning. These men I guess were in their 70s along with a few younger and "non-regulars" that would join the group. These generally 6 to 10 men would sit on a couch and chairs in a semi-circle. In the winter time they would circle part way around the wood burning stove. McFarland's store contained a small grocery area and restaurant counter where one could be served one of Mrs. Mac's dinners or desserts. When I was elementary school age I would go there with my dad because he liked to play nickel a game Pitch (cards) in a room in a back corner of the building. I would usually sit on a chair on the edge of the group of men and listen to their conversations. These men as they engaged in storytelling and good-natured kidding laughed with and at each other. All either were or had been farmers and had obviously experienced significant changes in farming including the transition from the use of horses and mules to mechanization involving tractors and combines. The men I remember the most clearly each had a particular characteristic to include a pipe smoker with a permanent indentation at the corner of his mouth, a growth of whiskers short of a beard, the user of a cane and a story teller. I don't recall anyone seeming depressed or complaining about medical issues. If one had complained about a minor ache or pain he might have been subjected to harmless kidding. Regardless, I thought they were old as I tried to imagine what that must be like and took some pleasure in thinking that I was far removed from that state. I was mostly ignored although some would say, "Hi Larry," at some point. I would return the greeting by calling that person by his first name. It did not seem right to address one of these familiar men as Mister. I would listen intently to the stories and their occasional jibes or kidding. At times later in life I have wished that I could find some way to recapture their social intercourse.

The farm where we lived was about a mile west of Bendena in this small rural community. And although Bendena was unincorporated with probably less than 100 people it was no sleepy little village. It had 16 different businesses in 1950 including a Studebaker dealership. The area was inhabited by community minded people that knew everyone else in the community. Churches were important with a Lutheran Church in town that my family attended and a Catholic Church in the country about 4 miles southwest of Bendena. There was a monthly community meeting of programs of music and skits with a dance. Neighbors helped neighbors when there was a need. Because there were no more than 30 students in high school, including only 21 my senior year, I was expected to participate in all school activities. These included all athletics, county spelling contests. school plays and singing as part of a duet. Although the limited curriculum was an eye-opening disadvantage when I went to college, I believe, however, I was ingrained with the importance of getting involved. Bendena High School closed in 1958 after consolidating with 3 other schools of similar size.

I am not certain how much the men at McFarland's influenced my thinking about being old. Among grandparents, only my paternal grandmother was alive and then only in my early years of growing up. She was probably in her late 70s when I was no more than the age of 7 or 8. She seemed old to me and not exactly warm and fuzzy. I later remembered or realized that her life had not been easy: that included giving birth to 12 children that lived to adulthood. I believe I learned from the men at McFarland's the importance of humor and relationships regardless of age. Although I addressed no one as "Mister," I recognized the principle of respect for the elderly and the

119

gems of wisdom that they would quietly or casually share. If I was spoken to, I would listen and probably nod and never think about interrupting.

The major influences during my youth that affected my attitude and behavior during all of my life involved my parents, particularly my mother. My mother was kind, gracious and positive. She was a hard-working farm woman that found time to tend to a big garden and a yard full of flowering plants. She would cook sumptuous meals for as many as 10 men during silo filling time and be active in several church and club activities. She loved to shop and felt an obligation to help others in the community in the way of providing transportation and doing visits. I never once recall her indicate that she felt cheated because her father had died when she was one and her mother passed away when she was 7. Because she and 2 older brothers lived with a housekeeper and later an older sister, I never thought of her as an orphan until someone recently mentioned this to me. Rather she found humor in life and laughed easily even when others did not.

She would laugh in her later years when reminded about the time she washed out my mouth with soap for expanding the normal language of a 5-year-old. I have little doubt that I was influenced by her genes and her example. Dad's attitudes were shaped by growing up in a large family of limited means and the Depression of the 1930s Although Dad never talked about it, I know he was grateful for his success as a farmer and cattle feeder. His common sense told him that success in life including happiness was not guaranteed. To support this, he turned down offers from newspapers and maybe magazines to do feature stories on his cattle and crop farming operation. He was a man of integrity and had absolutely no tolerance for what he viewed as irresponsibility, along with liars, braggarts and bullies. My parents rarely lectured me but I understood their behavioral parameters and expectations. Two of their greatest gifts were believing in me and giving me responsibility.

I had an older brother and a younger brother and sister. We 3 brothers slept in the same bedroom (in a 5-bedroom house) with me sharing a bed with my older brother. Yes, we teased and fought but I believe inherently learned the importance of compromise, sharing and working together. Every morning before school and regardless of weather, we had to get up and do chores, related to feeding 700 to 900 head of cattle. Being made to do things that were not comfortable or convenient was common and never questioned. I attribute being a light sleeper and waking up quickly to those early morning calls to get out of bed.

My belief is I started with the right genes and through life's experiences was "conditioned" to never let myself be too unhappy outside of tragic happenings. I think closely tied to the latter have been the qualities of adaptability and tolerance. Manifestations of this are the fact I lived in Vietnam for 6 years under challenging albeit rewarding conditions and in my late 60s and 70s, lived alone for 11 ½ years in apartments in the Washington D.C. area. Most of my professional career after Vietnam was disappointing and non-productive, at least in my eyes and in comparison, to my expectations. My brief and ill-fated venture into an entrepreneurial activity and subsequent 12 years in real estate told me that neither my interests nor talents lie in these areas. In the case of the former my judgment was questionable as well. These latter periods involved mostly frustration and questioning on my part, but I don't believe I was depressed, with one exception that I discuss below.

Although I was disappointed, I found ways to gain satisfaction outside of the work place through church and club activities in the community in which my family lived. Critical and underlying my attitude was the giving of unequivocal priority to our 2 children. I now take some satisfaction from my last job in Washington, D.C. where I administered the Refugee Agricultural Partnership Program, a new and successful program in the Office of Refugee Resettlement with close ties to the USDA. This job helped me rediscover the importance of relationships and treating clients and administrators at all levels with respect by listening to them and acknowledging that they had knowledge and insights that I did not have.

I have had many and varied experiences since Bendena. My 6 years in Vietnam were poignant and life changing. After working in agriculture for 2 years and 4 months, and 3 months of travel and home leave, I returned to Vietnam with the U.S. Agency for International Development (USAID). I was assigned as one of 44 senior civilian advisers to a province chief under the Vietnamese Pacification Program. The USAID Vietnam Program was the largest U.S. supported civilian effort in its history and I presume still holds that record. In Vietnam I learned or had lessons reinforced that included humility, the importance of understanding culture and history, respect for their knowledge and decisions and supporting the idea that they were responsible or had ownership for what took place.

In Vietnam, influenced by Chinese culture, the elderly are venerated. It seems in most cultures the elderly are respected and an important part of the growing up process for children. In some cases, this is because of the prevalence of extended families living together due to economic reasons and perhaps the cultural responsibility of parents to care for the grandparents. The quotation at the beginning of this writing was spoken to me in connection with marriage advice from Tommy Hsu in Vietnam. Tommy, a Chinese from Taiwan, who I believe was the best agricultural technician in Vietnam was probably in his 50s.

My experiences in life, particularly in Vietnam and later in refugee resettlement in this country, conditioned me to automatically compare my life and its blessings with those of perhaps 95% of others in the world. Working in Vietnam soon after college heightened my sensitivity and awareness of both life's fragile nature and preciousness. I once gave a ride to the home hamlet of a young woman with a baby after she and her child were delivered with her husband's casket via a C-23 to the local airport. The tragedy was not just her husband's death, but also the ominous future for herself and her child. A young girl maybe 11 or 12 years old died in the hospital after I witnessed her falling off a wagon of wood and being run over by one of the wheels. Because of nothing comparable to an ambulance service, a person with me and I had delivered her to the Nha Trang hospital. Besides tragic events among Vietnamese families I had people close to me that died prematurely. An education volunteer in his 20s that I shared a house with for a year was shot and killed by a squad of the Viet Cong. The closest friend I ever had and with whom I also shared a house in Vietnam for 18 months died of a rare form of Lou Gehrig's disease in his 50s. About a month before he died, I visited him and his wife for the last time. His once athletic body was gaunt, a shell of its former self, and he could not speak. Two of my better college fraternity friends both died at about age 30, one from a SAC airplane crash and the other as the result of a car accident.

I admit to thinking, "Why not me" and "Is being my

friend a curse of sorts?" In other words, I have felt fortunate or blessed. This is particularly so when I incorporate my own experiences. These include during summer break from college driving a tractor (in neutral) off the side of a steep hill and ending up only with bruises and as a non-swimmer having rushing water above my shoulders during the onset of a flood in my assigned provincial capital in Vietnam.

I also have reflected on unfortunate events closer to home including the early death of relatives and other friends. On an occasion after I took early retirement from the government and felt rather hopeless and sorry for myself, my attitude was changed by a simple conversation. The man of an older couple told me that their only child, a son, was killed in a car accident returning home from college before Christmas.

I am grateful for good or otherwise memorable and meaningful experiences in my life. My work in Southeast Asia allowed me to do things 55 years ago that are now rather commonplace. In the 1960s I visited the Taj Mahal, Angkor Wat, the Acropolis, Bethlehem (on Christmas Eve) and other historic places. I shared a hotel room in Athens with a man who later became the first president of the Country of Namibia. As guest of the engineer, I rode for at least 150 miles in the engine room of a steam engine train in Malaya. I feel that my life has been enriched by meeting and being friends with persons from a variety of backgrounds and beliefs.

By working in the domestic Refugee Resettlement Program for more than 20 years I heard and read about the traumatic experiences of refugee families. These included their witnessing of outright persecution and violence, (sometimes against family members), the loss of property

124

and homeland, and living under dire conditions in a refugee camp for up to 20 years. The latter and the Vietnam experience have resulted in an interest in international happenings and events. When I read or hear about the incomprehensible suffering in the world, I recognize how fortunate I and other Americans are. The stories are numerous and tragic and include places like Syria and neighboring countries, Yemen, the Congo and the Robingya from Myanmar. I have read statistics that say there are 22 million refugees in the world and 65 million displaced persons. By definition a refugee has been forced to leave his or her native homeland, and a displaced person is someone still living within the boundaries of their homeland. Fundamental to my thinking is the fact they are human beings who at one time had aspirations not too different from those of my own family, but now merely hope their family, particularly their children, survive and have a better life.

At an early age I think I subconsciously decided I wanted to make a difference in the world. I am not certain of the derivation of this, although I know I was influenced by my parents and the lessons of Sunday School. At age 81 I still have that purpose in life although I recognize my options are limited and how easy it is to be distracted by every day happenings.

I was probably in my late 30s and after I was the father of 2 children that I decided to give more serious thought to healthier living. My wife and I paid more attention to our family's diets even though it was far from being a model. In my middle 50s after I had left the federal government and started working in real estate I began walking 2 miles per day 5 or 6 days a week. Leaving the federal government was not a smart career move in terms of financial security but I was frustrated and finally said that life should offer more and that I had more to offer. Probably a positive outcome was it made it easier to start a walking regimen. I continue to walk including the 2.6 miles round trip to the grocery store and the 3.4 miles to the bank. If I don't walk, I pull on the $15 rowing machine that I bought at a garage sale. I no longer use the Nordic track or any of the exercise equipment purchased by my wife. I do yard work including mowing the lawn and cutting the shrubbery. I presume the combination of exercise, diet and genes have contributed to the fact I don't feel old or believe in most ways act old, but most importantly want to stay alive in body and spirit. I admit to comparing myself with others particularly of similar age. Maybe that is at least partly a matter of pride and therefore morally questionable, but I will live with this transgression.

I have come to believe that every person regardless of station in life wants to be treated with respect and dignity. I learned this early in life when hired men worked for us on the farm. In Vietnam I learned the importance of respecting its history and cultural values. The people I encountered wanted to be acknowledged and listened to. Most also found a way to have joy and humor in their lives.

I have both challenges and regrets. I was diagnosed with Addison's disease some 25 years ago. The main result of Addison's disease is a compromised immune system, however, I am rarely sick; I take daily cortisone pills and other medications. Thirty years ago, it was discovered I had serious glaucoma that had been misdiagnosed by an optometrist. For the past several years I have not driven a car. A few years ago, I developed rheumatoid arthritis and like many other older men I have prostate issues. About the same time as the onset of rheumatoid arthritis it was determined that I had a mild form of Type 2 diabetes. All of these can be frustrating but not depressing. I just tell myself that these are minor compared to the good things in my life and the life and death situations of many others. The bottom line is I don't feel sorry for myself or say "why me." I think I am inherently grateful for doctors and medicines. During my teenage years a favorite saying of my uncle and Sunday School teacher was "the sins of omission can be worse than the sins of commission." One of my omissions, or even failures, in life has been not to maintain relationships or stay in touch with persons with whom I have worked or become acquainted. My tendency has been to depart with expressions of gratitude and maybe much later wonder about how or what they are doing. When I worked at the Vietnam Training Center of the Foreign Service Institute in Arlington, Virginia in 1968, an older person, who had just returned from an assignment in Laos, told my discussion class of mostly young foreign service officers that they should keep a book of persons in their lives with contact information. This was mostly in the context of these individuals perhaps being helpful to their careers at some point. Regardless, it was advice that I hope 1 or 2 of my students followed even though I did not. In terms of my overall regrets I hope that later actions have made up for my mistakes and misdeeds. I also believe in grace and forgiveness.

My diagnosis of Addison's Disease in 1993 and the long-term prognosis associated with this were additional motivating factors for me to remain healthy. For most of the time since I have maintained a rather consistent pattern or regimen, although I know I could do better and may need to at some point. I admit to ice cream being the favorite thing for me to consume and that desserts like pie or cake left around the house have a short life span. Consequently, for the most part we don't buy these things. I try to read about the healthy foods in various publications and have a pretty good fix on what the "good" foods are. For example, I eat cooked oatmeal sprinkled with cinnamon and blueberries most mornings for breakfast. I have tried to cut down on sweets and carbohydrates like potatoes and bread after my diabetes diagnoses. There are indications that Addison's Disease makes one more susceptible to diabetes. Regardless, my A1C has been in a range where I take no diabetic medications.

When I began working with refugees in the early 1980s, I became aware of mental health issues common to many refugee family members. We initiated some conferences and workshops to try to better understand and provide agencies with ways of dealing with mental health problems. A couple of things from this initiative hit home to me. First is the important connection between the physical and the mental. These need to be in sync because the status or well-being of one can affect the other. This seems rather logical, but I found out that this connection is probably better understood in Asian cultures than in the American culture. The counter balancing factor then at least was that even the slightest indication of a mental health issue in an individual was generally a significant stigma for Asian families and one they wanted to minimize. The bottom line is attention and priority needs to be given to both mental and physical health.

Long ago, I accepted the fact that not all of my life's goals and dreams would be achieved. I don't dwell on these mainly because of my blessings that include family and health. I also recognize that I cannot change the past. I believe in the idea that one should have at least one good belly laugh each day. I look for ways to add humor to things as long as no one gets seriously hurt. With respect to my family, particularly on my mother's side, fun or pleasure was garnered from playing a joke or trick on someone. I try to adhere to the simple idea that you do not take yourself seriously, but you take your work (or actions) seriously. My son inherited this quality and once fed me a dog treat immersed in barbecue sauce when I was engrossed in another activity. I laughed with him, just not as hard, and my only regret was I had not played the trick on him. I like to think I am a reasonably good joke and story teller. These are important, particularly involving one's self, because they create a human side and makes people laugh.

At the risk of embarrassing the person(s) with me, I like to engage strangers in conversation. I can usually determine the persons that might be open to conversation. The results usually include learning something interesting and in many cases finding out we have something in common in our backgrounds. An added benefit is it also makes time waiting in places like a doctor's office seem shorter.

If it wasn't for things like calendars and birthday events, I would not know I was 81 years old. In fact, I deliberately do some things that are out of character for someone my age. But I am also aware that calling yourself or appearing old can at times be an advantage. Other than getting discounts on purchases people can just say something like, "aw, he is just old." But I have to admit that I get a little miffed when someone that I think must be older than me refers to me as "young man." Recently, I told someone that I knew I was old because on the same day this old codger referred to me as "young man" the waitress in a restaurant called me "honey."

I can still hold up physically to strenuous activity, just not as long. My wife and I just built about 250 feet of picket fence, but not just in one or two days. When my daughter got married about 7 years ago, at the wedding dinner she and I danced the swing or jitter bug to "Bugle Boy." a well know song during World War II. I concede that the people there standing to watch and the subsequent ovation were good for my ego. I am confident that I still have the "beat" and life in my legs to do that today.

I confess it was at least partly ego when I decided earlier this year to participate in a senior men's basketball session at the local community center. I was the oldest present among 10 or 11 men that met on the basketball court. All of the others had apparently been playing for at least awhile and in some cases also at other venues. After the second time participating, I decided my victory was just in trying. My basketball skills had eroded more than I thought as highlighted by just abruptly stumbling and falling to about an inch from kissing the floor. On the opposite team was a 6-feet-8-inch guy who had played center for Hank Iba at Oklahoma State. He was a gentle giant, but his extra weight gain from his playing days made him a formidable foe. I quit after 2 weeks mainly because I was afraid of an injury that would interrupt my ability to otherwise exercise. I decided that I would merely resort to telling my friends that at age 81 I was able to get on the court and move my feet and legs.

I was reminded in August of 2019 of both my vulnerabilities and capacities to do certain things. On a trip to Vietnam with my son and daughter I fell flat when I stepped sideways off a curb in Hoi An. My son remarked it was a positive sign that I was immediately able to get up without injury. I took some satisfaction in that we stayed in a different hotel room each of 11 nights. Beside the physical requirements there were the mental aspects of determining the different ways of opening doors, turning on the lights and getting water out of the shower. I dealt with an overnight train trip from Hue to Hanoi as well as my offspring did. Going through the Ha Long cave was a mixed bag. I was grateful for my exercise routine back home when I had to walk up 80 to 100 steps to reach the cave opening. My daughter and son took turns holding my hand and providing guidance along the darkened and uneven rocky route with several openings and short distances of no more than 4 feet high. Afterwards, I felt that I had met my exercise quota for the day. I would have failed or at least struggled getting through the several airports if it had not been for my daughter who recently returned after working in Africa for several years. Her familiarity with the various electronic and other procedures, including 5 or 6 "interdictions" in Los Angeles resulted in us not missing any flights.

The trip to Vietnam with my son and daughter was meaningful but not quite the same as I had envisioned. In one sense it felt like I was in a country for the first time because of the dramatic changes that have occurred. Maybe for this reason I had a difficult time connecting my experiences of 50 plus years ago with the new Vietnam. I also recognize that over the years I have reflected back thousands of time to Vietnam, particularly with respect to the people and the relationships. The latter undoubtedly contributed to my ability to retain much of my Vietnamese speaking ability. I would also tell the people in Vietnam this was because of my tinh cam (emotional feeling) for Vietnam. Upon returning to the U.S.A. in late 1967 it seemed re-adjusting to this country was comparable in difficulty to my initial adjustment to Vietnam.

131

It was emotional the morning after our arrival in Ho Chi Minh City when a now 70-year-old man met us with his 2 youngest daughters. He was a member of a small Montagnard Tribe (Raglai) and the only person from that tribe in secondary school when he lived with me in Phan Rang from 1964 to 1967. Thanks to him we were able to connect some 5 years ago and now do regular Skype calls. He was then and now a wonderful person who is active in his Protestant church when reportedly only 1 or 2 percent of Vietnam's inhabitants are Protestant. He traveled with the 3 of us for the first week of the 11-day trip. A highlight of the trip was sharing a lunch with his wife, three other daughters and son-in-laws, and 4 grandchildren in his home along the central coast north of Nha Trang. The day before his two younger daughters rode a bus the 150 or so miles from Ho Chi Minh City to celebrate my son's 48th birthday. They were able to bring a cake to a remote and rustic lodging accommodation and we celebrated his birthday at 9:00 o'clock in the evening under a gazebo like structure.

In several respects I have not had time to fully process the events and impact of our Vietnam trip. It is an understatement to say that the reunion between my friend and me was a happy one. Not surprisingly, after 51½ years Vietnam is not the same country. There has been tremendous growth and development. The three places I lived in Phan Rang are now unrecognizable having been replaced by newer structures. An exception to focusing on the new and not reflecting on the past occurred in My Nghiep Hamlet where Cham women still weave tapestries and decorative pieces on hand looms. Three of the women there remembered me because I would visit My Nghiep. Ba Noi, their aunt, was the "broker" for the tapestries in the 1960s and would come to my house. The three nieces took us to see Ba Noi who is now 90 years old; however, they were not sure she was able to recognize me.

The people, at least in the service industry, are the same, friendly and gracious. In some areas my adaptation to the challenges of the Vietnam trip was easier than those of my offspring. I sanctimoniously made an issue of both of them ordering a pepperoni pizza in Hue, the home of supposedly delicious and unique foods. I think I may have compared it to ordering a hamburger in New Orleans. Anyway, after repeating my disappointment and admonitions a couple of times, my son took offense saying something like that at age 48 he didn't need me telling him what to eat. This frosty period did not last too long as my daughter explained that in walking by the kitchen the day before on the way to the bathroom in Hoi An they had made the mistake of glancing into the kitchen of this local restaurant. As a result, it was decided they had consumed enough Vietnamese food for a couple of days. We took the 12 plus hour overnight train trip from Hue to Hanoi. Unlike them I thought the accommodations including the bathroom were all right. I had not really noticed but they both objected to the bay window between the bedroom and the shower room in the nicer hotels. There were blinds but the silhouette was a bit revealing. Our guide took us to a quaint coffee shop in Hanoi and suggested we try this special kind of coffee. The prognosis was generally favorable until one of my traveling companions found out from reading the label that weasels were a part of the processing. I finally decided that maybe I had carried my qualities of tolerance and adaptability too far. I also concluded that I had instinctively compared accommodations with those of 50 plus years ago when in most of Southeast Asia there was one bathroom on each floor of a hotel and the walls had holes in them. The above do not account for the good times when the three of us enjoyed culture, history, incredible scenery and yes food. I was honored that my son and daughter were unwavering in their desire to visit Vietnam with me, the place of life changing experience and memories.

I admit to now having less patience and tolerance and the fuse to my anger button burns more quickly than several years ago. I don't know if that is a telltale sign of being old and more judgmental or having the benefit of more experience. I am not sure why I do not participate in social media. I rationalize this by some combination of thinking that I have more important things to do, a preference for face to face interaction, and I don't need Facebook or Twitter to be happy. I don't care for fads or things to which I believe I will not sustain, such as specific diet plans. My "technological" skills have yet to be developed. A person close to me once said that I had the technological aptitude of a gnat. When I asked this person if these could be upgraded to those of a fly, my request was denied.

I do believe that life should be a continuous process of reflection and learning. I reflect on things I did as recent as 5 or 10 years ago and think, "Boy that was stupid" or "why did I do that." But I try to learn from my mistakes and am not afraid to give consideration to different ideas, to include some writings, the content of which I disagree.

I attend church regularly. In the last several months I have started going to a men's discipleship group. My wife and I attend a small Bible study group of couples. These groups have been good opportunities for learning and reflection and have been enjoyable due in part to the other participants and the camaraderie. Like in my youth I believe the teaching of the Bible should influence my behavior.

I take pride in having many friends or acquaintances with diverse backgrounds and ways of thinking, although I have few in which I feel comfortable in confiding. This is probably an area in which I wish I had a higher score. One of my best buddies runs around our house on 4 legs. And although our dog is not one in which I can confide, she is always friendly and forgiving. She enthusiastically welcomes me when I return home from being gone for just a short time and reminds me when it is time for her to eat, go for a walk and visit the backyard. For these reasons and because she listens to most of my requests and commands and takes advantage of being spoiled, I believe she is intelligent. Yes, she is an important contributor to my happiness and contentment.

On TV I watch mostly news programs and sports, the latter related to my 3 favorite teams, although admittedly there is a correlation between their winning and my time spent watching. Regardless, I follow my teams and get emotionally involved during games. I also read TIME Magazine, a daily newspaper and a few other publications. In terms of publications, health related articles usually grab my attention. I try to stay abreast of particularly national and international news. In terms of national news and events I often find myself amplifying and expanding on the words and phrases for which my mother washed out my mouth with soap. I am certain she is disappointed but hopefully understanding. I am also frustrated with the international news. Besides the political saga(s) I cannot fathom the amount of violence, suffering and death that millions of people endure. Overall, the magnitude of man's greed and selfishness is staggering. At the same time, I recognize that there are multitudes from all levels that dedicate themselves to doing good works.

I occasionally think about, but not dwell on, the issues of our country and the world. These are numerous and collectively overwhelming, and in my opinion do not bode well for our children and grandchildren. But any reflection and despondency relative to these things are short lived. I presume this is because I have chosen to try to be happy in life and have hopes that ways will be found to solve or ameliorate these issues.

I do occasionally think about what my life could be like as I get closer to dying. Incorporated with this is the question, "what is the best or least of the worst ways for this to happen?" My wife and I have spent money on long term care insurance, but I have visited enough nursing homes to hope that this is not in either of our futures. This combination of thoughts, however, do not occupy much of my time at this point. As the old farmer might say, "I still have some ground to plow."

From writing and reflecting on the above I have come up with the acronym ADAGE that fits or captures my thinking. The first A is Attitude. My attitude starts with not wanting to die yet, staying positive and still wanting to make a difference. D is for Diet. I am far from perfect in this regard, but I try to eat some healthy foods and not go overboard on the unhealthy. The second A represents Awareness. This is difficult to define but it has been important for me to think about the people and events that have affected my life. I also believe that maintaining an understanding and knowledge of local, national and international news provides a perspective on my own life. For me it opens the door to understanding and relating to others. Genes represented by the letter G is the one thing we cannot change, at least not yet. However, by following the other things represented by these letters we can significantly obviate the impact of the chromosome material we inherited. The letter E stands for Exercise. I would sometimes prefer to skip my walking or using the rowing machine, but I usually proceed. Regardless, I am able to enjoy good health because of an active life style. I think my exercise is a key to me still being alive in body and mind. If I could find an acronym that could also accommodate another D, I might add the word Discipline, one of my favorite words.

A few years ago, I reflected on the lessons I was exposed to growing up on a farm in Kansas. I grant that then in particular I did not understand or adhere to all of these items. However, I believe many, if not most, of these lessons were absorbed into my being and were reinforced through my life's experiences.

Farm Raised: Lessons Taught, But Not Always Learned

1. Telling the truth means you never have to lie.

2. Being given responsibility makes for confidence and being responsible.

3. Stop working when the task is done not when you feel like quitting.

4. Hard work does not mean having no fun.

5. Every person regardless of status wants to be treated with respect and have a sense of dignity.

6. Regardless of status you pitch in to include a willingness to get your hands dirty to do what is necessary to get the

job done.

7. You learn discipline and perseverance by doing or being made to do things that are difficult and/or you don't like.

8. Modesty wears better than any sign of arrogance.

9. Not remembering the old mistakes of others wipes the slate clean and opens the door for a new script.

10. Helping a neighbor is a natural choice.

11. Keeping a count on the good deeds of yourself and others is not necessary.

12. Challenges and difficulties make you smarter and stronger.

13. Sunday is a day of rest, worship and/or reflection.

14. Making a big deal out of every incident means you have misplaced priorities.

15. Laughter, good times and fulfillment do not necessarily require the spending of money.

16. Honesty is not a trivial pursuit.

17. Religious affiliation does not determine the measure of a person.

18. To understand the lives of others creates a perspective on your own life and its vulnerabilities.

19. No lessons are more profound than the ones learned from experience especially the bad ones.

20. Laughter even at unexpected times serves as a salve and opens the windows to your personality.

21. People will respond generously to genuine needs but are turned off by what appears to be irresponsibility.

22. An inner peace and appreciation of nature are felt by walking solitary through a timber.

23. Efficiency and organization are habits that can save time and reduce burdens and stress.

24. Being able to anticipate and plan is the foundation of organization.

25. The abilities to adapt and improvise increase your capacity to make adjustments, deal with adversity, be more efficient and have less stress.

26. Showing respect and listening and adhering to the words of one's elders result in learning and the establishment of a bond with bountiful memories.

27. Make a habit of returning an item to where you found it to avoid wasting time the next time you need it.

28. Include yourself as being responsible for what happens in your community and the world.

29. Raising one's voice is seldom necessary unless there is an emergency or the person to whom you are speaking is across the pasture.

30. The ability to analyze, gauge and accept the results related to risk builds perspective and judgment.

31. Determining a reason for doing something good or potentially positive is better than finding a reason not to do it.

32. Having the biggest and/or the most expensive is not always the best.

I had other experiences during my growing up with individuals who at the time were or seemed elderly. If nothing else these experiences have caused me in my later years to reflect on these. It was my mother that encouraged me to visit the neighbors on the farm immediately to the west of us. At about age 6, my initial ride on Tony, my pony, across the field to meet Grandma and her son and daughter was the start of a regular pattern. Grandma was not really my grandma and in fact she had no real grandchildren. Neither her daughter or son, probably in their late 50s, had ever been married. Grandma, maybe close to 80, was warm, gracious and very much aware of the world around her, but always needed the use of a wheel chair. Their modest home had no indoor bathroom. They would always ask about me and my family and would share interesting stories. Grandma, known as that by people in the community, along with her son and daughter, attended the rural Catholic Church about 4 miles southwest of where they lived. My mother would comment on how Grandma was such a fine Christian person. About 6 years after I first met her and she was in the last few days of her life, Grandma asked to speak to me in her bedroom. I do not recall her exact words except that I remember her gently admonishing me in my life to do God's will.

Although they seemed older, they were probably in their 40s when I first met them at the Lutheran Church my family attended in Bendena. He was crippled and had a rather severe speech problem supposedly from being dropped as a baby. His sister, slight in stature, was the ultimate caregiver and would put her arms under his shoulders as he would shuffle his feet in order to move. Before the days of ramps being common, she would lift each of his legs up each of the 10 or so steps in order to get into the church. His mind was sharp, and he would mix in a hearty laugh in the midst of his broken speech. On the other hand, her demeanor seemed to reflect her difficult and challenging life. She was quiet and unsmiling and often did not enter into conversation unless it was to interpret his speech. They had lived in the community with my mother and her family for many years and would express their admiration for her. Sometimes at the end of church my mother and I would go to where they were sitting to speak to them. He had a story he often told with loud laughter about my mother's reaction to when he referred to my older brother as "Jumbo" when he was a baby. I visited them in their modest home a few times when I was in high school and college. They were avid readers of the Bible and on occasion would talk about their faith. They were vehemently against alcohol. When I was in Vietnam, I received a letter from him that I do not recall answering, a regret of mine.

I am not sure how much my experiences with the 2

families above affected my attitudes and behavior during my lifetime. I am confident that I added a measure of happiness or pleasure to their lives with my visits and our interactions. The first family could tell me how much they anticipated and appreciated my visits. In the second family, he was always engaging and liked to share his thoughts and stories. I wish I could have done better as I think of other persons that were limited in some way and/or isolated. My wish also is that young people and others will consider joining persons already engaged in doing visits as a way to add comfort and pleasure to someone's life. It might be uncomfortable in the beginning but the pleasures you provide and the learning you experience will be your reward.

Larry Laverentz grew up on a cattle feeding and crop farm in Northeast Kansas. After graduating from Kansas State he worked as an agricultural volunteer in Vietnam between 1961 and 1963 with International Voluntary Services, the organization the Peace Corps was patterned after, In 1964 he joined the U.S. Agency for International Development and served as the senior civilian adviser to the Ninh Thuan Province Chief in administering U.S. support for the Vietnamese Pacification Program.

Subsequently, he held various positions for 20 years in federal programs including refugee resettlement and other social service areas in the Kansas City regional office of the Department of Health and Human Services. After early retirement from the federal government in 1991 he worked as a real estate sales agent for 12 years. In 2003 he began working as a contract employee in the Office of Refugee Resettlement (ORR) in Washington D, C. With ORR he was the first program director for the Refugee Agricultural Partnership Program. He retired in 2014. Larry has a Master's of Public Administration from the University of Pittsburgh. Larry and his wife live in Lenexa, Kansas, a suburb of Kansas City. Their son is the pastor of a large church in Edmond, Oklahoma and their daughter has recently returned to the Kansas City area after serving as the Chief of Party for a major health project in Ghana.

okay

Pat Laster

On Living a Long Time

By

Pat Laster

In mid-July 2019, Martin Samuel's online opinion in the *Daily Mail* was headed, "For goodness sake (sic) Federer is 37 and too old to be doing this." It caught my eye, first because my sister is a huge Federer fan and second, the man was urged to quit at the age of 37!

The second paragraph read, "And momentarily, the spirit sagged and the limbs creaked and the old man looked on the point of surrender . . . From somewhere, again in the ether, a fresh energy inspired him, the years tumbled away and [he] played . . . the greatest, most focused tennis of his twilight years. If these indeed are his twilight years."

Yet on MSN Sports, the *Miami Herald's* writer, Greg Cote's headline read, "On the brink of history, Serena [Williams] goes for all-time record in Wimbledon final." Cote never uses the word "old." He begins with her debut at age 17. Today, at age 37 (38 in two months hence) has won 23 tennis majors. Now, at Wimbledon, she wants a 24th career major singles win to tie the all-time record of Margaret Couch in a 1977 career end. Though it's Serena's sixth attempt, she's lived through pregnancy, birth of a daughter, and a pulmonary embolism. She's been trying since then "to prove she has another—or two—in her." Twenty-one years of working toward her goal and not one word about her being old. Bravo! to Greg Cote!

Another article posted after Serena lost her 24th win, written by Ben Weinrib, Yahoo Sports contributor, said ". . . Her 2017 win at age 35 made her the oldest to ever win a major title and she became the oldest player to ever compete in a final . . . Williams may no longer be in her prime, but that's still good enough for #11 ranking in the world."

Bless Mr. Weinrib's heart! Not one pejorative due to her age. By the way, these two stories are an example of the woman being treated better than the man. It's also an example of differences in sports writers' attitudes.

Social media is good for laughs at the expense of the aging. From Soulseeds this: "Most people don't think I'm as old as I am until they hear me stand up." (Shared by R. Roberts and P. Longstreth.)

Another, this one from the famous and wonderful and long-lived Betty White: "I have no regrets at all. None. I consider myself to be the luckiest old broad on two feet." (From the New York Post, January 17, article by Rob Bailey-Millado)

Paul Longstreth, Houston Texas, shared this quip from the site Lessons Learned in Life, Inc. in mid-summer 2019: "I'm at the place in my life where errands count as 'going out.'" Granting his permission to quote this, he said he'd be honored.

Closer to home, Ginger English, a local writer, photographer, grandmother, wife, etc. posted on her Facebook page one mid-summer day, "You never know when it will strike, but there comes a moment when you know that you just aren't going to do anything productive for the rest of the day. That moment just struck me." I read it around ten a.m. and the post had been up for two hours—on a Saturday! She also gave permission to quote her.

Another social media post, this one from Casual Christian Comedy: "I don't let my age define me, but the side effects are getting harder to ignore." This was shared by peers slightly (only slightly) younger than I. (The site had no listings for rights or reprints.)

Here is a paragraph I transcribed from Ray Bradbury's book, Fahrenheit 451, p. 156 – 157:

"Granger stood looking back with Montag. 'Everyone must leave something behind when he dies, my grandfather said. A child or a book or a painting or a house or a wall built or a pair of shoes made. Or a garden planted. Something your hand touched some way so your soul has somewhere to go when you die, and when people look at that tree or that flower you planted, you're there. It doesn't matter what you do, he said, so long as you change something from the way it was before you touched it into something that's like you after you take your hands away. The difference between the man who just cuts lawns and a real gardener is in the touching, he said. The lawn cutter might just as well not have been there at all; the gardener will be there a lifetime.'"

When one reaches 80 one wonders what will be left behind when one moves to that Final Address. The Bradbury paragraph describes it as well—or better—than any I've found. I also have heard that as long as anyone remembers you, you live on.

Oh, I know lots of folks 80 or older—and thank goodness, a lot of them are my friends and relatives: Uncle Norval, Jimmy Carter, Dot, Freeda and Gene, Bettye and Betty, Ted, Cordell, Nelda, Faye, Pat, Patti, Jean, Doris, Sue, JoAnn, Phil, Birma, Cathy, Sissy, Johnny, Charlie, Holland, Carolann, "Red," Jim and Versie, Anne, Shirley, Beverly, Barbara, Curtis, Virginia— which includes my own high school classmates, who are now nearly—if not all—83.

But 80 is so young!—comparatively speaking. I remember back a-ways, reading a book that began—and I paraphrase— 'She was an old woman of 60'. I was livid! How dare an author make such a statement? How young must the writer have been? But on second thought, I wrote this senryu a few years later: "66th birthday/ driving across two states/ and feeling my age."

But at 60, I was single and raising a six-year-old grandson. We moved to another county to take a new job, which meant finding a home, getting belongings trucked down, meeting neighbors, work colleagues, school folks, and those at the courthouse. It meant locating the post office, the grocery store, the school, the church, the print shop, the gas station, the school-uniform outlet—no activity for an "old 60-year-old," right? Wrong.

Living to be 80 and older is, as they say, a luxury that a lot of folks don't and won't ever enjoy. But of all these people I've named, not one of them is sitting on the porch swing or in the rocker feeling sorry for themselves. (Merriam-Webster has added the non-binary pronoun "they" to its dictionary, according to CNN online.) No, most of them are busy volunteering, care giving, going to church, attending activities at the senior citizens' center, weed-eating, mowing, walking, serving on committees and boards, making plans to travel, beginning new projects. One I know has been accepted into an online graduate program to earn an MFA (that would be me).

And each of us will leave behind "a child or a book or a painting or a house or a wall built or a pair of shoes made. Or a garden planted." Or a book published. (Or several books published.) Or a smile given. Or a hug. Or a kiss.

As a young 83-year-old, my fourth book, A *Compendium of Journal Jottings: A Sourcebook for Writers* has been published (by Cahaba Press, no less) and available on Amazon. On Labor Day, 2019, I hosted the 65th reunion of the Bryant High School class of 1954.

Two more poems of mine on the subject: A cinquain, "Living Longer" (from an obit in 2006) "Dying/ 70 years/ to the date of his birth—/ Yesterday, I turned 70/ also." And, "For the First Time" I felt/ old today. I/ felt as if I walked like/ an oldster. At 82, I/ *am* old!"

And may we live and thrive—like some in the above list, and like both my parents did—to 90 and beyond.

And BOO on the one who opened his book with an old woman of 60!

Pat Couch Laster is an Arkansas native. She earned a B.A. from Hendrix College and a M.Mus.Ed from University of Arkansas in Fayetteville. She did graduate work at San Diego State College and is presently enrolled in an online MFA program from U of A at Monticello. She taught public school music for 27 years, and Gifted and Talented classes for part of the final four. In 1984, she enrolled in a graduate class in Gifted Education, "Writing Across the Curriculum." It changed her life. The writing bug bit. She's been schooled in "lucid" poetry, under the tutelage of Ted O. Badger, long-time editor and publisher of *The Lucidity Journal.* For many years, she has been a workshop leader at the annual Lucidity Poetry Retreat in Eureka Springs, AR. She was mentored from afar by the late Robert Speiss, long-time editor of *Modern Haiku,* who published the first poem she sent him. In 2013, she was appointed poetry editor for *CALLIOPE: A Writers Workshop by Mail,* published four times a year from Green Valley, AZ. In the late 1990s, in addition to raising a grandson, she published a year's haiku flip calendar with Dorothy McLaughlin of New Jersey and since then has produced myriad monthly haiku booklets. A novel and a sequel were followed by a collection of short stories and long poems, *Hiding Myself into Safety.* Only recently has her fourth book, *A Compendium of Journal Jottings: A Sourcebook for Writers been published by Cahaba Press.* Her present projects are a memoir, *When I Had Another Name* and a poetry collection. Presently, she is a member of LBJ&P, a writers group that meets monthly to critique, to share and to encourage each other. She has attended Hemingway-Pfeiffer Museum Educational Center's writing retreats in Piggott since 2006. Each spring and fall, she is a resident at the Writer's Colony at Dairy Hollow in Eureka Springs.

Blogs include: pittypatter.blogspot.com—poetry, and pittypatter-pittypatter.blogspot.com—prose. Her website is www.PatLaster.com.

Some stuff is interesting,

Some not — irreverent

? ?

Dan Krotz

Be Nice. Don't be a Dick

By

too long

Dan Krotz

I've been taking a furniture making class from a guy named Sam Davis. As a young man, Sam was a carpenter, and then he became a contractor who built homes and home additions. Following an accident, he became a science teacher and then a teacher of teachers. Now, Sam is an artisan working in areas such as drawing, stained glass and, of course, furniture making. He specializes in "legacy" furniture, which is stuff with a story attached that you hand down to your kids and grandkids. An example is of a couple who took a walnut tree from the family farm and had it milled into boards. Then they asked Sam to construct a bench the couple will leave to their heirs "when the time comes."

I've never made any legacy furniture, but I have made hundreds of benches—and probably more than a thousand "farm" tables—out of recycled wood. Recycled wood is discarded lumber that started its afterlife as privacy fences, barn walls, and as decks off the backsides of McMansions in tacky taupe housing subdivisions. I'd see boards in dumpsters and start diving, or pass by a house going up (or down) and ask the contractor if I could clean-up the scrap. They always said yes.

My wife, an antiques dealer, painted and distressed the benches and tables I made and sold them to women with "shabby-chic" decorating joneses and subscriptions to

Better Homes and Gardens. My sole interests in slamming this crap together was to make my close with a dollar wife happy and because I like recycling. Observing, feeling, and smelling wood were unintentional but pleasant consequences derived from my scrounging, but these were always secondary to the governing motivations.

When my wife retired from her business as an antiques dealer my services as a furniture maker were no longer needed. That was fine by me since "slamming this crap together" accurately describes both my work ethic and skill level. When Sam suggested I make a couple of "legacy" benches for my kids I, without much thought and in an entirely haphazard manner, agreed because I enjoyed imagining my kids remembering dear old dad when they glanced at their benches.

I like Shaker furniture. It is simply designed, functional, and quite modern in appearance. I bought two 8-foot yellow pine 2x10s for $30 dollars, and agreed to take a couple of classes from Sam to knock out a pair of identical Shaker benches. Seven months later, I'm sort of close to finishing them. Kind of close. Maybe.

What began as an introduction to furniture making has evolved into a period of reflection and a better understanding—better defined as a series of rational and moral judgements—of the kind of person I am. Summarily, while using a Japanese coping saw to cut dovetails, I discovered that I'm a half-assed, thoughtless, and not very bright guy. My woodworking class has been, by outcome if not by design, self-admission to a virtual psychiatric hospital where I'm self-evaluated for a raft of character disorders.

This period of introspection was not caused by instructor Sam. Sam is focused on the process of making fine furniture. He never explicitly invites introspection. But Sam is a perfectionist while I'm habituated to "good enough". Think Zen Master and Grasshopper...and on the moment when Grasshopper realizes a grasshopper is an insect.

My confinement to this psychiatric facility of the mind has occurred during the same time I had a birthday that, by any measure, is Old Age. Let me admit to being in a state of shock at being not only old, but at the sheer volume of evidence leading to the verdict of Old. I am falling apart in the way that Hemingway's character Mike Campbell described going bankrupt: "Slowly. Then all at once."

No, I'm not dying of anything specific, but I'm clearly dying, if not tonight then sooner rather than later. The clarity of entropy is simply more pronounced than it was (or could be) at any other period of age.

If you Goggle "thoughts on old age" you're directed to websites like BrainyQuote. These sites list dozens and sometimes hundreds of "wise" and inspiring sayings about how to be old, what being old is like, and even why being old is synonymous with being cool. Of course, there are some grumps in the crowd. Mason Cooley said, "Old age is falling asleep at the funerals of your friends." And then there's Philip Roth: "Old age isn't a battle. Old age is a massacre."

Roth's summary lacks precision. Old age is generally a series of skirmishes, then a battle, and only then a massacre. Notably, precision may not be possible because everybody lives and dies in their own way and only after a period of time measured by luck and chance. "Lifestyle" certainly plays a part, but lifestyle (choice) is more often driven by factors of either or both nature and nurture—luck and chance in other words.

Obviously, I have been thinking about being old, with an emphasis on "being" as a thing with potential. I'm not worried about being's correlative opposite—nothing (death)—except for aspects of the process of becoming nothing. By "aspects of the process" I mean the usual stuff: inconvenience to myself and others, pain, embarrassment, boredom, dependence, etc. Like everyone, when I go, I hope to go quick and not dirty.

The idea "you're only as old as you feel" has some substance, but it can also be evidence that the idea's owner is ignorant of self, or even delusional. The common example is of the elderly driver who causes accidents because of age-related deficiencies but still thinks he's A.J. Foyt.

I don't particularly differentiate between professional decline—too old to practice medicine, teach, drive a truck, etc.—and the generalized decline that is inevitable as we march from being to nothing. It's possible, perhaps likely, there isn't anything to differentiate: decline is decline. Yes, we grow richer in experience as we mature. But maturity is accompanied by the loss of innocence, for example, and perhaps our sense of wonder. That's mostly a fair trade, but at what point does experience become mere remembrance, or pantomime? Retired people can grant themselves a free mental-health pass as they dodder around the house, but self-ignorance or delusion are factors that must be periodically addressed as we (and others) assess our professional competence, whether we're pitching baseball or running for president.

Compensation is also a useful tool for old people. Some of us can pay people to do what we can't do anymore. For example, I've cleaned my house gutters for the last time. Next year, I'll hire someone to do it. Similarly, we compensate for decline with canes, with walkers, with pills and Viagra until, at some discouraging moment in the too-near future, there's a conversation with the kids about moving into a nursing home. For someone who vividly recalls Peter Fonda and Dennis Hopper in *Easy Rider*, the idea of living at the Shady Rest is a lot scarier than that Greetings! letter I got from Richard Nixon. Compensation is useful, but it can be a kick in the ass too.

Decline can be compensated by improvements in areas where we can still improve, such as our moral behavior, civility, and sociability: we become better people. These can be small changes. I make a point of smiling at (nearly) everyone I run into these days, whether it's in the soap aisle at the Evil Retail Giant or at the check-out window at Mickey Dee's because it makes me feel good when people smile at me; I decided to return the favor. And I spend dreadfully boring hours every week taking a cranky old bat to the grocery store and doctor's appointments...because... you can't actually be a good person unless you do good stuff.

Improvement opportunities can also be challenging. I moved from a Top 10 State (Minnesota) to a Bottom 10 State (Arkansas) for better weather, and without thinking about the considerable cultural, social, and political differences between the two places. Minnesota certainly has cold winters, but it also has effective state and local governments and progressive politics, and a generally well-educated, healthy and productive citizenry. Arkansas does not. Instead of discovering and enjoying the many good things about my new home, I spent the next two decades focused on the seamier aspects of its people, appearance, and operation. Oh Lord, I was stuck in Lodi.

I wrote two novels documenting my misery. One, *Coffee*

with John Heartbreak, described the virtual imprisonment of a cranky old bookseller staring out his shop's windows at the comings and goings of his mostly illiterate Appalachian American neighbors. *Semi-Faithful: More Coffee with John Heartbreak*, attended on the local evangelical culture and moral character that predominates in the South generally, and in Arkansas particularly. Without putting too fine a point on it, the Bad Catholic John Heartbreak found a culture focused on blond Jesus and the Arkansas Razorbacks challenging.

I'm not sorry I wrote these novels, but at the time of their writing I wasn't near the end of life with pre-paid cremation services with the local undertaker. I'm not a visitor anymore. Now, I concretely accept that Berryville, Arkansas, is where I live and it's where I'll die. "You better cheer-up, Fat Boy," I said to me. "You don't have a lot of time left."

Cheerfulness is not one of my attributes. I come from a long line of Norwegian and German depressives who personify the meaning of existentialism. If someone made a movie of my family lineage Ingmar Bergman would be the right guy to do it. I see him framing a shot of a fumbling drunk with his nose perched on a glass of beer at the end of a dark bar. Bergman would title the scene 'Krotz's Grampa…and his Grandpa's Grandpa.'

Compensating for Nature's unfortunate gifts takes many forms. That may be why so many comedians are depressives, why introverts join book clubs, and why fat people diet, lonely people buy dogs, and alcoholics join AA. Comedy, clubs, diets, pets, and abstinence are all strategies for improving on what can be debilitating character and natural challenges. My own "the glass is half-empty" world view was appreciably helped by logotherapy,

160

a form of existential analysis developed by Viktor Frankl, the author of *Man's Search for Meaning*.

"What is to give light must endure burning," Frankl wrote, to explain how empathy is possible only when we expose ourselves to the trauma and suffering of others. It was only when I put myself in the shoes of my neighbors was I able to (mostly) agree with Berryville's Mayor Tim McKinney when he said, "poor people and barking dogs got to live somewhere," as I complained about the city's lack of code enforcement.

What "giving light" means is offering a friendly smile to distracted shoppers at Walmart and resisting my compulsive urge to sit in judgment of the people and the place that surrounds me. Instead of making fun of them and it on social media, or in the columns I write, I'm trying to understand and accept them for whom and how they are. Some people may think this is irresponsible, and a retreat from holding basic standards, and they could be right. But my judgmental character has turned me into a sourpuss, and designed a squalid mess out of the world I've chosen to live in. I may not deserve better, but I want better, and better starts with me.

What does "starts with me" mean? Activism is one approach, one that many "old timers' can list in their resumes. Baby Boomers, by example, are foundational members of the anti-war movement. And in the fight for civil and women's rights. Volunteerism and philanthropy are other forms of being better. We see groups of people cleaning trash along our nature trails and river banks, for example, and many folks take the idea (value) of tithing seriously. The most basic form of being better is simply to do no harm. We may not clean up trash along the river, but at least we put our litter in trash cans and serve as that most annoying presence, a good example. Doing no harm and serving as good examples may be the most important among these starting points.

I'm not knocking activism, or volunteerism or philanthropy. But in a now long life dedicated to all three activities, I can't say my life, or character, was much improved by them, or that I made much of a difference. As I observe our culture, civility, and political and other environments as we near the end of the first quarter of our new century; I'm unable to say we've improved appreciably as a people, or as a nation either. We've got plenty of leaders and plenty of opinions on how the world should operate. What we don't have enough of are good examples.

Neither am I criticizing material or social success. It's okay to be proud of becoming self-sufficient, raising and supporting a family in comfort, obeying laws and social norms, and paying your taxes. But such behaviors and outcomes are what's expected of us; it's merely normal, not extraordinary. Unless you've discovered penicillin or been awarded the Purple Heart, all you've genuinely earned is a participation trophy. The upside, the Sunnyside of "just" normal, is that you've done no harm.

What matters most at the end of life is, frankly, the opinion we hold of ourselves. If we need the opinion of others to distinguish if our life has been worthwhile, that tells you everything you need to know about what your opinion is worth.

That self-opinion, and all compensatory improvements, depends, of course, on one's capacity for self-awareness, self-honesty and freedom from the delusion that one is an inherently stable genius with no need for self-assessment or improvement. It's easy, for example, to be a limousine liberal in a big city, or a Big Shot Critic in a small town, but congruence between how we behave and what we say is the ultimate measure of character. Tolerance and patience, acceptance and happiness, like charity, begin at home. I didn't know that when I moved to Berryville, Arkansas, twenty-plus years ago. I know it now.

The downside of such interior compensation is that self-assessment may lead to feelings of guilt or remorse, and perhaps depression, especially if one lacks the opportunity to make apologies or reparations because of death, or ostracization by other family members or groups who've decided to cut you out of their lives. We might call this emotional place "the region of regrets." It is certainly the place where we finally understand that behaving well is not only its own reward, but has long term rewards too. The aphorism, "if I knew then what I know now I would have done things differently," sums it up.

The experience of journeying into the region of regrets varies among people, of course. Guilt, in my view, is often a sign of good mental health because we can affect improvement or make amends only if we aspire to certain standards and have the capacity to identify right from wrong. Yet modern culture and its religious institutions—with a few exceptions—assuage guilt with what is fundamentally a prescription for narcissism, and ignore the fact that the narcissist's assignment of blame and self-centered personality disorder is always counterproductive. These are the people who rarely experience feelings of guilt—or authentic feelings. How can they, after all, improve on what they perceive of as perfection?

Every age group faces the challenges of warding off narcissism and engaging in self-improvement, but old people have less time and consequently fewer chances for becoming an improved human being. The assumption that "you're only as old as you feel" may express optimism, or it may be delusional. Most likely, it is both. That's likely why there's such a broad and diverse array of clichés (opinions) about what it's like to be old.

My turn in the woodworking shop, a.k.a. psychiatric hospital, produced lessons and learnings. With respect to the day to day stuff, or professional decline, I learned that I will never be a competent wood worker. My hands shake, I can't see or hear well, and I grow tired fast. I also learned that wood workers must invest thousands of dollars in tools, even if they are simple hand tools. If I live another 10 years—a wholly optimistic idea—I can't justify that expense, particularly since decline is apace: I will shake more, grow tired more quickly, and my hearing and sight will become worse. I will use these tools less and less and they'll end up being on that list of one more damn thing for my kids to discard or sell. What can't be sold or discarded, though, is that conscientiousness and attention to detail are characteristics of true love.

I also learned in a hands-on way to respect people who work carefully and thoughtfully, who are not driven by economy of scale considerations, and who refuse to become slaves to our mass consumption master. I, perhaps more than anyone, shouted-out to the ideal of small economies of scale, but never really understood that "small," as a business, craft, or career, legitimizes carefulness, high standards, and an appreciation for the idea that "a good place to make a living" is not equivalent to "a good place to live." Few people regret approaching a job with care and high standards. I suspect the same could be said for how we live.

Among my regrets is advising a client who made doors

164

and windows to modernize his factory. I told him to buy technology and machines to kick out "product" to meet European Union sizing standards. That would open up markets, primarily in Switzerland, for his doors and windows.

We were in the town of Gjakova, Kosovo, which had been ruthlessly bombed when Kosovo's ethnic Albanians sought independence from Serbia. I was a fat American getting USAID money to give expert advice. He was an Albanian-Kosovar who'd lost his wife and a brother in a bombing raid; his business, a small company started by his great grandfather, was also destroyed.

The war had been over for a couple of years, but Gjakova was still a mess. Dead buildings were piled into mass graves at the end of streets, and army jeeps—driven by Italian and German NATO personnel—patrolled the streets between the piles. The Italian soldiers were casually glamorous in sunglasses and flowing silk scarves. The Germans were grumpy and efficient and did the work.

The land around Gjakova is beautiful, primarily hills and valleys covered with chestnut trees interwoven into a network of fast running streams. I was reminded of the Ozarks when I looked at them.

My client, Melos—who's now a friend—made his doors and windows out of those trees. Before the war, he and his brothers used hand tools to shape the chestnut into doors and windows for primarily local markets. Today, a kid with computer skills programs a chain of machines to plane, cut, assemble, and glue the doors and windows into precise sizes. Melos and his brothers feed the machines and load "product" into trucks.

"I'm making money," Melos said, in a recent email, "and the Swiss are impressed. But I am a bit worried.

"You see," he continued, "the machines are thinking for me. And I no longer talk to the wood, or feel it or smell it. I lift it and shove it around, and I have no idea what the computer is doing. I have made the trees into slaves, and myself one too.

"I miss thinking and feeling."

There were other professional discoveries in Sam's workshop. Like Melos, I discovered my math skills are poor because I've come to rely on machines to do my calculating for me. I work on fairly complicated spreadsheets every day for business purposes and function like an accountant or financial officer to make decisions based on what results are produced by the spreadsheets I create. But I no longer know how to confidently use a ruler. How long is 25/32 of an inch? It's a hair over ¾ of an inch. But it took you a moment, didn't it? It certainly took me more than a moment because I habitually measure things in quarter and half inches. That's the tolerance standard—¼ inch—I used in the production of benches and tables for women with decorating addictions; close enough for government work ... and Krotz.

I can, even in old age, improve my skills for using a ruler. That requires an internal agreement to spend the time necessary to use a more precise ruler—32nds rather than 8ths or quarters—and to reject "close-enough" standards. And I agree to do that. That's the good news. The bad news is "close enough" is the standard I've chosen, not just for making tables and benches, but for how to live my life too. Why did I make that choice? Was it laziness? Bad character? Simple ignorance? Cultural and moral conformity? All of the above?

I'm afraid the answer is "all of the above." As I look back on life, I remember far too many times when I took the easiest path, was less than disciplined (sometimes disgracefully so), and worried too much about what other people thought of me. Sure, I'm describing not just myself here, but a common human condition too, yet I'm the guy who has to live with me. How did I end up this way?

When my mother was 18 years old, she met a 19-year-old traveling salesman who knocked her up on the edge of a cornfield in western Minnesota. They got married in Deadwood, South Dakota in November of 1948, and I popped out in March of 1949. I was joined by 5 brothers and sisters by the time my mother 27 years old. We lived in several different towns in Minnesota during that time, and in South Dakota, Montana, and in the big woods in central British Columbia, Canada, for three years. We moved around a lot.

When people ask what my parents did for a living, I always tell an old Abbott and Costello joke. "My parents were in the iron and steal business. My Ma ironed and my Dad stole things." In the case of my parents it wasn't really a joke. My mother worked as a waitress or kitchen helper after her children entered school and my dad was a cab driver, a welder, and a self-employed trucker and gas station owner. Toward the end of working his life he got a pilot's license and owned and operated a small under the radar airline company in south Florida that got to be successful transporting—according to my mother—illegal aliens and drugs from Central America. By that time, he and my mother had divorced.

Three experiences were life transforming for me. First, was when my family fled to British Columbia, Canada, to escape packs of rageful bill collectors. Penniless, we moved into a two-room log cabin with no electricity or indoor plumbing, and I was enrolled in a Catholic missionary school on an Indian reservation run by nuns from Ireland. All of the students at St. Joseph's Elementary School were Athabaskan Indians except for a handful of Portuguese kids whose Catholic parents had immigrated to BC to catch and gut salmon taken from the Nechako River. And then there was me, another Catholic kid, but one who could speak English, and read it too.

The nuns who ran the school had a tough job. They were far from home, barely out of girlhood themselves, and where supervised by a terrifying school principal who had been shuffled off to Canada by church superiors who didn't know what to do with a Very Holy Person who was visited by the long dead St. Theresa of Avila several times a day. In this setting, and among the Indian and immigrant students, the nuns decided I was superstar smart: I could read! I could speak English!

And I could read. A little bit. But because there was no television, and no radio, and absolutely nothing to do except chop wood to heat our leaky cabin, I discovered books and how they magically worked like first class tickets away from reality. Instead of watching my parents drinking and fighting, feeling cold and lonely, or worrying about the worms in my poop, I floated the Mississippi with Huck Finn, killed Mormons alongside Lassiter in Riders of the Purple Sage, and went to Africa with Martin and Osa Johnson. I had my 10-year-old nose in a book 12 hours a day, proof to the Sacred Heart nuns that I was a very smart boy. And since I was treated like a smart person, I came to believe I was one. School was a calm and much appreciated place for me and has remained that way until this day.

The second transformative event in my young life was helping my dad put new brake shoes on a '54 Plymouth parked out in the back yard. "Help" is a simplified phrase

168

here. My real duties were to watch and bear witness to my father's suffering. He didn't have the right tools for the job, and he didn't know how to do what he needed to do; and he was half in the bag, per usual. My assistance involved chasing thrown tools, getting cussed at for moving too slowly or clumsily, and hearing one more variation on the never-ending story of how he was the victim of ungrateful children, an ugly weepy wife, and Jewish bill collectors.

In the week prior to my help-on-demand brake shoe servitude, my 7th grade teacher, Sister Mary Paul, secretly handed me a copy of Evelyn Waugh's *Brideshead Revisited*. Her act was a secret because the book had homosexual characters in it and was thoroughly condemned by the Catholic Church. It was at the top of Church's No No List, right up there with John O'Hara's *Butterfield Eight*.

I don't know why Mary Paul gave me the book, but I read every word of it. Most of it was over my head, but the one big thing I got from it was that young men went to a place called "college" where they laughed, wore clean clothes, made friends, played games, and had an enormous amount of fun. I didn't know anything else about "college," but it sure beat the hell out of playing Step 'n Fetchit for the World's Greatest Victim. I determined then and there that I was going to go to college.

And I did go to college where the third life transforming event took place. I answered an ad for "roommate wanted" in the Minnesota Daily and found myself walking up 3 flights of stairs in a ramshackle dump where I knocked on a dirty brown door. It was answered by a guy named Rod Britton, who was just starting work on a Ph.D. in physics. If you can imagine Sheldon Cooper from the *Big Bang Theory*, minus Sheldon's social graces, you know all that's necessary to know about Rod Britton.

Rod was the consummate nerd, right down to the slide rule in his back pocket and plastic pen pouch in his front shirt pocket. He also played the accordion ala Myron Floren and was massively unsuccessful in his attempts to get a date—the only characteristic we shared. Where Rod was a brilliant mathematician with a profound knowledge of classical music and German philosophy, I was an eighteen-year-old social foundling who read Goethe but pronounced his name "Go-theee." Rod was also an atheist while I was still submerged in the tepid bath of self-loathing inspired by a Roman Catholic upbringing.

As socially inept as Rod was, he was Fred Astaire compared to me. Because of my father's misanthropic and violent behaviors, he was cut off from his family—and from my mother's family as well. My parents had no friends. Consequently, my brothers and sisters and I were socially and culturally isolated. While growing up, I never attended a baptism, a funeral, or even family or neighborhood picnics and get togethers. The first church wedding I attended was my own when I was in my mid-thirties. Because of our social isolation, everything I knew about behaving and interacting with other human beings came from the novels I read. I was, more than less, Mowgli with a library card.

Rod Britton took me under his wing. For the time we were roommates I studiously observed him interacting with his friends and peers—almost all of them graduate students in physics or mathematics—and copied their behaviors, right down to wearing plaid shirts and chinos while every other kid in America had flowers in their hair and covered their butts with bell bottoms. Rod was the guy who helped me pronounce Goethe's name—among hundreds of others—correctly.

It was my association with Rod and his peer group where I found and nurtured a class, social, cultural, and political identity. The anti (Vietnam) war movement raged across the United States at the time, and our conversations frequently focused on it. But within the group those conversations included references to Robert Oppenheimer and Niels Bohr, the House Un-American Activities Committee (HUAC), and our government's long history of persecution of activists and dissenters. By observing these conversations—I was really too ignorant to participate—I learned that everything is connected and virtually nothing happens by chance. Although Rod was only 8 years older than I was, he essentially became my surrogate father. From him, I learned how to interpret the world around me and how to organize my behavior within it.

There have been other transformative people and experiences in my life, but those three where foundational and eternal. I look back on them with both amusement and gratitude.

My Model of the Universe

Years later, when I was in graduate school at Hamline University back in St. Paul, Minnesota, Huston Smith, a visiting professor, assigned his students the task of designing a Model of the Universe. Smith, a philosopher and Comparative Religions scholar, wasn't interested in planets or how to measure the speed of light. He wanted our best guesses about how we—meaning me, the Big I— saw the world and our roles within it. I drew a bicycle wheel. If you will, please imagine that wheel as we read on.

At the center of the bicycle wheel is a hub. The hub is the

171

center of the Universe. Springing from the hub are spokes. Note that the spokes close to the hub are close to one another. As the spokes leave the hub they grow further apart, yet they remain connected by the bicycle wheel's hub and outer rim.

The center of the hub is where the Universe's "organizing principles," originate. These principles, or rules, may be God, a code of conduct, a value system, what we learn and know, or simply an overall philosophy of life. Functionally, they are one or any combination of higher powers that guide how we operate and systematize our lives.

Higher powers can be as complex and perplexing as the Judeo-Christian deity, or as simple as a parent we may be afraid of but who we also love and trust. Love is the important part of a higher power's composition because love is enduring and (relatively) stable. There are, for example, lots of "higher" powers in our lives who we fear but don't love. These can be the bosses who sign our paychecks or cops who, when we see them, cause us to slow down or fasten our unbuckled seat belts. But when cops are out of sight they are also out of mind. True higher powers are with us always.

I'm a spoke who springs out of the hub and into the wheel's rim. So are you. You and I are 2 spokes out of 7,000,000,000 spokes. The spokes next to us—closest to us—are the people who usually share the same or similar organizing principles and what are called "institutional constructs." The people are usually family members or friends, and sometimes a hero who serves as an example. The constructs can be religious denominations, schools, branches of the military, fraternal organizations, and so on. I was raised as a Roman Catholic, attended the University of Minnesota (Ski-U-Mah!), served in the US Army, and belong to the Sons of Norway. Consequently, I am closer to the people—the spokes—who share those institutional constructs with me than I am to, oh say, Southern Baptists who root for the Arkansas Hogs, dodged the draft, and are card carrying members of the Southern Heritage Society.

Spokes are spokes—and human beings are human beings—because we emerge from the hub and travel toward the outer rim of the wheel. Such travel broadens us, and we—some of us—grow rich in experience, mature as we age and, while we remain closest to the people and constructs most like us, we, just like the spokes in a wheel, grow further apart from other spokes as we become individuals.

Every spoke—every human being and all living things—sooner or later arrives at the bicycle wheel's rim...where we all get connected again. The rim is death. Death is what connects us.

What happens after birth is or can be documented. You can make a movie or write a book about it...just like this one. But what happens after death is a matter of faith or opinion, both of which are hard to document. Long ago, and before our present era of political correctness, the Principal of my elementary school, Mother Gonzaga—or Ma Gun, as she was accurately but not affectionately known—would stand by a classroom window and swat flies.

"Another dusky Hindu bites the dust!" she'd exclaim after every successful swat.

Ma's PC deficiency was invested in the Hindu idea of reincarnation after death, of which she was obviously making fun. Meanwhile, she overlooked her own afterlife adventure where, as a "bride of Christ," she anticipated a hot night with Jesus. My own favorite is the 7 (or is it 70?)

virgins all good Muslim men look forward to.

Religious people like Roman Catholic nuns, Hindus, and Muslims have their own particular or generalized idea of what the rim is. Some call the rim Paradise or Heaven and many of them believe all God's children got shoes because God is that ultimate tautology, Great and Good. Father Divine, an African American evangelist, told his followers they'd all be driving Cadillacs in Heaven. For an all-powerful (Great) God, a Cadillac is just as easy to hand out as a pair of sneakers. God is Good because He's Great and God is Great because He's Good…and around and around we go.

Among the 39,000 Christian denominations there are at least as many conceptions of what happens "inside the rim." My own spoke's pathway from hub to my presence at the edge of the rim has converged from a six-year-old's belief that Jesus would give me a Moon Pie for breakfast every morning, to my being okay—this morning—with drifting up from the roots of a tree and into its leafy canopy before release into the ether. If there is any consensus about the rim of life, it's that you're dead on arrival. That's when we "all" become "one."

How we understand the afterlife is organized by our belief in some sort or set of higher powers. At birth, that higher power is the mother's breast. Nature (genes, intelligence, physical appearance, personality—good or bad luck, in other words) and nurture (family money, loving and close parents and relatives, being born in a safe and civil country of origin and available support systems—again, good or bad luck) are the starting points that take us beyond mama's breast and shapes how we discover and experience our higher power. Values and consequences are inherent characteristics of experience. As children, experience is influenced by family, playmates, school, church and temple, culture, and rules.

As adults, our childhood values (may) change as experiential consequences result from interactions with family, friends, our education, religion plus or versus philosophy, and culture, co-workers, and the law. Somewhere along the experiential trail—the spoke's pathway—we become responsible for nurturing ourselves. Our natures, on the other hand, continue to function as independent contractors. Some people are born on third-base. That's nurture. But it is nature, as opposed to nurture, that permits third-base residents to conclude that s/he's hit a triple.

Nature and nurture play a part in our openness to new experience. Some people spend their whole lives living right next to the hub before shooting off quickly to the rim. These are folks who never, for example, leave the small towns they grew up in, stay deeply invested in the churches they were baptized in, and so on.

It's absolutely possible, of course—and true in my experience—that lifelong small-town Baptists can possess broadly and deeply comprehensive intellectual lives. Anyone can, for example, get a Harvard education at the local public library if they're born with intelligence and curiosity (nature)…and if their library invests in good materials and their parents instill within them a love of reading and learning (nurture).

What isn't likely to happen at small-town public libraries are encounters with Jewish vegetarians, Surfer Dudes, very Hot Chicks with Ph.D.'s in Mathematics, or meeting up with Trust Fund Babies who can't decide whether to spend the summer with mom and dad on Cape Cod or go to Aruba with friends. The small-town Baptist isn't likely to rub shoulders with Transcendentalists, Rastafarians, Stoics, out of the closet transsexuals, pansexuals, bisexuals, homosexuals, or well-adjusted celibates in cassocks. If they live in Louisiana or Mississippi, chances are good they won't even know a Lutheran. Oy vey, as they say (but not in the South.)

Provincialism and dogmatism are often consequences of a life spent close to the Universe's hub. These attitudes can, I assure you, throttle opportunities for the maturation and wisdom that come from experience, adventure, and self-discovery. On the other hand, G.K. Chesterton said, correctly I believe, that "Dogma is not the end of thinking. It is satisfied thinking." Some things are rationally and morally Good ... and some things are not. That's why an amoral jerk is an amoral jerk whether he lives in a big city or a small town: his organizing principles—the values and codes he carries out from the hub—are flawed.

The worth or usefulness of organizing principles depends on their accuracy in evaluating the journey from hub to rim. Individuals who are character disordered, such as sociopaths and psychopaths, are unable to rationally or morally evaluate themselves—or others—because Nature has soured their characters with toxic and ingrained doses of impulsivity and self-interest. Their organizing principle tells them they are, for all intents and purposes, their own God, and when they are rebuked or punished for their pathologies, they become misunderstood victims unfairly treated by freakish authority figures.

It's within everyone's Nature to have streaks of pathology built into their character. And everyone has behaved impulsively and in self-interested ways. But unless Nature hamstrings our innate character with thicker than normal streaks of pathology at birth, Nurture assumes the

176

major role in how organizing principles regulate and structure our childhood and adolescent interactions with the Universe. The values and consequences inherent in experience shape these organizing principles as we age and become adults. This is true for big city hotshots who've traveled the world, and for small-town rubes who inherit their dad's Phillips 66 station and never leave the counties where they were born.

Our organizing principles construct two standard measures used to evaluate ourselves, others, our histories, and our present environments. These measuring standards are rational and moral judgement.

Rational judgements are facts. "You are wearing a red shirt" is a rational judgement (if, in fact, I am wearing a red shirt). "You are wearing an ugly red shirt" is a moral judgement. I may think my red shirt is beautiful, and I could go on and on about how wonderful it is, but you, fashion Nazi that you are (oops, I've morally judged you), think my red shirt makes me look dumpy, fat, and old. So, is the shirt ugly?

Here's the rub: I look dumpy, fat, and old in and out of red shirts. I look dumpy, fat, and old in white shirts too. And in green shirts … and … shirts, obviously, have little or nothing to do with how I look. Moral judgments, about shirts and everything else, are obviously subjective and depend on rational judgments for evaluating whether we— and anything else—are banal or irritating, charming or dull, or…Good or Evil.

Let's beat this dead horse a bit more:

A red shirt is red. It may be a light red or a dark red; it may harbor shades of pink or orange, and to the colorblind fella it may even be gray. But run the shirt through whatever mass spectrometer clothing manufacturers use and 99 out of a 100 people will stack it on the red shelf. That's because red, in all its various poses, is basically red.

Ninety-nine out of every 100 people leaving the Universe's hub will also identify red shirts as red. It only gets complicated when those 99 people morally judge—subjectively evaluate—the red shirt.

How do humans make moral judgments? This is an unresolved debate, and with good reason, because moral judgments aren't just opinions. They're the decisions we use to send people to the gas chamber, pick who becomes Prom Queen, and decide if it's okay or not okay for the First Lady of the United States to be an East European hooker. Given their weight, moral judgments are often assumed to be rational.

The 10 Commandments are good examples of how moral and rational judgments become entwined. There is broad consensus that killing another human being is bad (Commandment 5: Thou shalt not kill). We don't routinely kill one another because it upsets civic and personal functionality. In fact, we feel so strongly that killing another human being is bad we'll kill you if you kill someone. And from time to time we've killed people if they didn't believe in the 10 Commandments. Or for putting their feet on private property without permission, for being a Communist (or a Capitalist), or if their mother is a Jew. Obviously, the devil—perhaps literally—is in the details.

Concluding Unscientific Postscripts

I've told you a bit about my travels along life's spoke and described how I think the world operates now that I've reached the Big Wheel's rim. Noticeably, I've decorated those travels and observations with moral and rational judgements about the person I was then, and how I became the person I am now. Those judgments have resulted in a list of conclusions about that life now that I've actually lived one. It's a short list; but allow me to present it in what Kierkegaard would call "Concluding Unscientific Postscripts."

An important concluding postscript is that organized religion is valuable because it lays out basic ground rules for how mankind should behave in order to assure basic civil rights. Beyond that, it has done more harm than good. It primarily functions as a tool to avoid existential realities and to facilitate control of lower social classes by monied or power-hungry elites. I conclude that any God who simultaneously needs and demands my love and approval is too insecure to be an actual God. It is, of course, possible that I am wrong, and this God will condemn me to an everlasting life in the fires of hell because I have failed to honor His insecurities. As far as I'm concerned, that God isn't welcome in my house.

That aside, I am in favor of church membership and regular attendance at services because it helps meet the basic and foundational needs of human beings to be social creatures and civil operators within their families and communities. While I am no longer a practicing Roman Catholic, I emphatically acknowledge that the Catholic Church was the single stabilizing influence in my otherwise chaotic and routinely brutal childhood. While I now believe, from the perspective of an old man of some experience within it, that the Catholic Church is a devolving cult that often warps and deforms hearts and minds, I am grateful for the structure and protections it afforded me long ago.

Along those lines, Sinclair Lewis wrote, in *Elmer Gantry*, that churches are often the only place in small towns where "you can hear the best music, see better art and architecture, learn about great ideas, and discuss the higher philosophies." As a regular church goer, I've found that to be largely true. Church is also a place to witness and measure the passage of time: little kids grow up and marry, old folks fade away, and seasons unfold and fold. We mark and are marked by the passage of time in our churches—and we and our fellow members witness such markings.

If these churches stick to nurturing civic and social order with messages of love and duty, and do no harm, may they live long and prosper. Otherwise, they're simply, at best, a division of the entertainment industry or, at worst, a racket.

Another concluding postscript, clearly unscientific, has been my youthful and middle-aged error in assuming man would evolve into an ever more civil creature because of advances in science, education, and economic equality. Much of that assumption was grounded in my experiences as a member of the Catholic Worker Movement, as a life-long pacifist and anti-war activist, and as a member of the Baby Boomer Generation—that generation dedicated to "peace, love, and rock and roll." Little did I imagine the anti-war (Vietnam) movement would peter out when the draft ended, or that a plurality of Boomers would agree to do just about anything for money. Frankly, I am deeply embarrassed by how little my generation has contributed to our political and civil order, and how our "right" to pursue happiness has avoided any engagement with the responsibilities that are central to the exercise of those rights. In some ways we Americans have made progress as a civilization and democracy—I think of the gains women and the LGBT communities have earned—yet more and more of us have simply evolved into monkeys with guns. I recognize this conclusion sounds nihilistic, and perhaps it is. Yet, I am satisfied that doing no harm is of greater benefit to society, and to mankind in general, than is most activism. In my opinion, it is far better to refrain from buying a plastic bottle of water than to expound high and mighty thoughts on the dangers of global warming.

The adventurer, brain surgeon, and rock musician Buckaroo Bonzai once said, "Wherever you go, there you are," a quotation I've annoyed my daughter with since the time she was 10. I like it because it concisely summarizes a brutal truth that is both advice and admonition. The advice is to make the best of what you have. The admonition is to stop whining.

As a kid who's understanding of the world was through literature, I grew up thinking the common and often mundane daily life most of us live was actually a poorly written novel with a boring plot. While books—or movies or TV series like *The Desperate Housewives*—can be fascinating and even life changing; they are not alive and they are not life itself. Regretfully, I failed to heed Buckaroo's counsel, too often focusing on the downside of my various physical environments and neglecting seeing and valuing the day to day world immediately around me. This unscientific postscript concludes with the instruction to myself to cheer-up and be less judgmental of the lifestyle choices of the Appalachian Americans who surround me. This instruction is useful to you too, whether or not you have AAs in your life — and yes, I'm laughing at myself.

My final concluding unscientific postscript is that we've confused our ceaseless consumption and perpetual comfort with happiness. By no means do I denigrate money or spending it on things that make us feel good. But ceaseless access to, say excellent coffee, or the perpetual warding off of cold or hot weather because of ubiquitous central heating and air conditioning systems, permits us to take for granted what were once rather special things. Striving for "better" is certainly natural, but when better is easily obtained we lose the feeling of gratitude, the essential foundation of happiness. Arguments against the bounty of modern life are wrongheaded for sure, but we haven't figured out yet what the cost of losing a grateful heart may be. I hope we realize what that cost is sooner rather than later.

What have I learned in my nearly eight decades of life? Slow down. Have more sex. Take care of your teeth. Be nice. Don't be a dick.

Dan Krotz is an author and semi-skilled intellectual who lives in rural Arkansas with his wife Susan. He is a father, a taxpayer, a veteran, and does not have an arrest record. When he is not drinking coffee, he mows grass and walks his dog

Dot Hatfield

Maybe Someday I'll Retire (Again)

By *okay*

Dot Hatfield

So, they gave me a Lifetime Achievement Award. What exactly does that mean? Congratulations, your career is over? You've done well, but you're getting pretty long in the tooth? You need to quit? I don't think that's going to happen.

It doesn't bother me for people to know my age as long as they don't categorize me for it. I was the middle kid of five. All through my childhood I heard that I was "too young" to do the fun things my older brother and sister were doing. Or, that I was "too old" to enjoy the pleasures that fell to my younger siblings.

Age has nothing to do with it, folks. I'm a living example of that.

At age 55 my husband and I took an infant grandchild into our home because his mother couldn't take care of him. We were empty-nesters. All the children in our blended family were grown with babies of their own. What were we thinking? Weren't we too *old?* Would we have the stamina, good health, *patience* to take on the stages of child rearing? Do the math. When he hit the rebellious teens, we'd be in our seventies!

We found daycare and I fell into the role of a working mom. Up at dawn to shower, bathe the baby, pack a diaper bag, get myself ready. Husband would feed him breakfast, deliver him and pick him up from the La Petitte near his work.

This became our routine as the baby grew to be a toddler, kindergartener, second-grader. Then, as happens in life, I unexpectedly and unwillingly assumed the status of single parent when my husband suddenly died. What we had agreed to do together, I was left to finish alone. I found a school where I was able to take him with me in the morning and pick him up from after school care.

There were playdates and PTA, report cards and Christmas programs, day camp and sleep-away camp. We played T-ball and learned to ice skate. Ask me if I know what a Power Ranger is. We struggled through math every year. My prayer was that I would live at least until he finished high school. That prayer was answered with a bonus of ten years (so far).

My acting career began about the time I became a senior citizen. As a fundraiser, our church produced a summer dinner theater — *Joseph and the Amazing Technicolor Dreamcoat,* and I was in the chorus. Since then, I have been in 25 productions, playing roles of every size and range of importance. Didn't someone say "There are no small parts . . ."?

I played Mrs. Paroo in *The Music Man* when I was sixty years old. The part calls for a woman in her forties. I simply died my salt and pepper hair auburn and no one knew the difference. Or maybe they suspended disbelief. At age seventy, I played ninety-something Aunt Florence in *Leading Ladies.* Most recently (at age 85), in *Cemetery Club* I was Doris, who dies quietly in her sleep.

I began writing fiction in my early sixties. I had long been a diarist and through my day job had written corporate

186

newsletters and press releases. Also, many scathing letters to the editor that were never mailed. The local community college offered a class in fiction writing and I said, "Why not learn something new?"

The responses to the short stories I entered in regional contests gave me all the encouragement I needed to continue writing. My one-act play was produced at Center on the Square in Searcy, Arkansas. I submitted articles to national magazines and anthologies. I found that I love to write but I hate to market my work. As of 2019 I have published four novels, one collection of short stories and a collection of essays from my blog, dothatfield.com. And of course, the play, *R.I.P. Emma Lou Briggs.*

About the time I began writing fiction, I retired from my dream job at a counseling center in Nashville, Tennessee and moved to a small town in Arkansas. My 10-year-old boy would be in smaller schools and I would be near siblings. The church we joined (United Methodist) offered classes for lay servants. That sounded like something I would enjoy, so I enrolled.

After a year of retirement, I felt a financial need to go back to work. My employment career had been mostly in the non-profit sector, most recently in a crisis counseling center. A local agency advertised for a person with writing and editing skills. Even though at that point I was not published, I applied and, *thankyoulord*, got the job as assistant to a Literacy Specialist in an Education Cooperative.

The grant was for three years. That was in 2001, but here I am still supporting other specialists (after my first boss moved on) at the same cooperative, which is located one mile from my home.

During my lifetime, I had two long marriages. One ended

in divorce and the other in death. Neither ending was less painful than the other. But, Ed, my second husband, was my cheerleader. He encouraged and supported every new thing I tried. Bless his heart.

I'm here to tell you that you are never too old to begin a new hobby, a new vocation, a new relationship. There are no age restrictions on learning, serving humanity, or falling in love. I'm proof of that.

Let's recap. Since becoming a senior citizen, I have retired and gone back to work, relocated to another state, bought a house (on a 30-year loan), become a Certified Lay Servant and Speaker in the United Methodist Church, and adopted my son. I have published seven books and written over 300 blog posts. I am working on a memoir (probably unpublished) for my children, grandchildren, and greats. I received an Archie, Lifetime Achievement Award, from Center on The Square Theater group in Searcy, Arkansas. But that career isn't necessarily over. Just wait till the right part (a very old lady) comes along. I'll be up to the challenge.

If I had my life to live over — I definitely would.

Dot Hatfield is Mom, Grandma, and (Great) Grandma Dot, who started writing seriously about the turn of the Century (2000). Her short stories and articles have appeared in several state and regional publications. She has published seven books. Her latest novel, *Worth the Candle,* was released in January 2019. Dot lives in Beebe, Arkansas, where she is active in church and community projects. Visit her blog at *dothatfield.com*

Adrian Frost

13 Cantos

By

Adrian Frost

Read two pages, don't leke the language (handwritten)

Every time you read; you're talking with the dead…
…and if you listen, you might hear prophecies.

~Kathy Acker

Remember Hamlet? Where a bunch of players turn up to act the play that allows Hamlet to launch the javelin of his inquiry into his father's death at his mother hand, thus precipitating the tragedy?

Well, this piece of writing has that drift. We come across a touring band of players, traveling as they have, before cinema, before theatres over all parts of our planet, Japan, China, Europe, Africa, to tell our stories, to try to understand our dilemma and indeed sometimes with Moliere to encourage us to roar with satiric laughter at it; at us. If this were a film, you'd hear the drums and a few half-assed bugle warm ups. Sorta like an early New Orleans funeral parade.

The actors, a motley crew on a good day are half drunk half daft and half anything else you'd care to mention; as in half-hearted half chanced half dead half a moment, they have been employed to be a funeral a lament a dirge. As far as I know they were hired by someone pretending to be a dude name of Jehovah. So, their play is a funeral and they don't know who's in the coffin, they think he/she was old and possible venerable.

Ps: they've already been paid, always a mistake but don't ask me about it, Jehovah paid. Thirty pieces of silver down and every month a payment comes into the far-gone wells of contrition vaults *wiv ole jee ha hovas* signature on it.

The actors every month religiously send film video of the traveling funeral to Heaven's Gate where the checks R cut and sent to them care of ole Gabriel's pony express.

CANTO 1

Voice over
Disembodied woman's voice over the sound of
the traveling players' oxen drawn
Funeral theatre cart

".... quicker diagnostics
Then a few years ago
Glad for you have kids and grandkids
So good reason to stick around and see."

Male voice
(That appears to be issuing from the coffin)
"Yo Eurydice
I have to be
Honest
I'm not here to be a grandad
I'm here to be a bad arse
Artist
The games up I bin working in the recording studio since 7
am

It's not a boast just a fact I'm on the way to 4score years
and I've
Got some songs hardly begun
I meet people who tell they've
Retired
But are full time grand
Parents
Fuck that
Not interested
And that awful bitch of an obituary
" he died surrounded by loving family"
Makes me puke
I far rather dye in a run-down brothel
On the boarder drunk with the goddess Buddha
Sporting my last fine upstanding boner
From hell
Shit somebodies gotta say it
I might wish I was at least being
Satirical
But I ain't
Female voice
Ha I can visualize that
Male voice
Good cause I'm
Gonna film it
And have it played
Loud and distorted
On a fucked up
PA at the rehearsal for my Funeral pyre

Last shot
We see the players go 'round a bucolic bend
Dust coming off the oxen's hooves

193

And the wobbly cart wheels
A weeping willow above the departing
Cart
the coffin looking suspiciously like a makeshift metal
garbage can to me ...
Fade to Billy Holiday's Devine voice singing weeping
willow.

CANTO 2

Chorus
Oh as I was young and easy
In the mercy of her
means
Time held me green and
dying
Though I sang in my chains like the
Sea.....
We see Richard Burton up on the screen
Chanting Dylan Thomas's song
Close up of him looking down fern
Hill his face changes to its ten
Year old welsh boy approaching adolescence
Then into him playing
Mephistopheles
Each line of the song his physiognomy changes
Into his other selves .....

Next up on the screen
Ever - Un - Knowable & Un-
Struck -Sound
Are just getting out of
Bed

Un -Know-Able
Says
Un- Struck -Sound I dreamed you were giving
Me Buddhist head .....

Meanwhile back in the garbage bin masquerading as a
Coffin
Scumbag wrapped in a Yu Wippi[7] blanket smelling of
Hound
In the funeral cortege, red dust billowing off the wooden
iron rimmed wheels
Of the cart
As it passes by the trail side weeping
Willow
Billy Holiday's voice runs cross the prairie
Sage up into the hills Purple in the
Setting sun

CANTO 3

We see the 12 Lotus Petaled
Heart Chakra inscribed on the inside of the garbage can lid
which is the cover for the makeshift
Garbage can, coffin Scumbag is presently in wrapped in
the yuwipi odor of hound smelling blanket.

Chorus
The actors are dressed in Elizabethan costume because they
were going to do Hamlet
Before that guy called
what was is name again?

---

[7] A shape shifting blanket.

For the last time *jeee hoooo vahhhhh*
Right *jeee ho vah*
(unbeknownst to the crew Jehovah is trying to get rid of his
doppelgänger
Be L Zee Bub in a burial disguised as theatre)
Scumbag who has been smuggled out of the jail in the
garbage bin got
Loaded onto the passing players wagon and for his Sin(s) is
playing Beelzebub?
He doesn't know whether he's playing him dead, alive or as
a ghost, or indeed who he's playing, he just knows he's
gotta play dead to, get his sorry ass outa solitary
confinement
PS. we're looking for the director of this film whom I hope
we meet soon when he realizes who he
Is
Billed HolyDay climbs up onto the back of the cart/stage;
she's all wet because she's just got out of her tin, (floating
with pulled daisies) bath, fully clothed, where she was
method acting Ophelia.

I can tell you for a start Ophelia ain't goin to no nunnery
dead daddy or no dead daddy and my ole hammy boy
being close to being king ain't gettin me there neither
She sneezes
Not happening I'm freezing from laying in the water
pretending to drown and now we ain't doing the scene

Oh, shit sister just do the action and read the lines
says Thanatos who looks suspiciously like Marlon Brando

I thought you was Eros
says Ophelia

I'm playing them both
says Brando

I thought ole Siggy Freud was playing one of them
He doesn't have the voice he can't act to save his Oedi Pus
and he don't have the Hollywood look
we've put him back working on the script

So, what do I do now
she asks?

Pick up that shovel over there by the open grave; watch that
skeletal head (all ass poor Yorick)
And now give the garbage bin lid a good whacking and
then make your inquiries and remember it's a funeral not a
fun fer all
Sez Bando

Act I scene I
She looks most fetching doth Billed Holy Day , the
Elizabethan dress so form fitting because so bath drenched
as tight and showy as a wet t shirt contestant

Get thee to that garbage bin coffin an play a rousing
medley ont
growled Marlon,
whose lit a cigarette and looks exactly like Stanley in
Streetcar

Ophelia HolyDay plays a rap raps on the garbage can lid
with the grave diggers shovel with the sacred heart Chakra
emblazoned Under its lid
Sparks fly

She turns
The sun setting red back of her shoulder
The birds, high above her head in the evening sky
Swarming about to seek roost for the night

She sings;
she has a voice that can raise the dead and put hungry
babes to sleep
It kinda blue you can hear Lester Young's horn prowling
beneath such a voice

Hey You you; You a livin yeh you you a livin
Or you jus playin dead
I said you/yeh you/a You a livin or you jus plain
Dead .....

I wasn't that comfortable jammed into that
Bin
But I involuntary begin to
Sing
To be 'onest I can't
Say
Wever I'm Livin; livin or
Dead

Why can't you say why can't you say why why oh why
can't you say

Billie sings suddenly like a Wagnerian opera singer Loud
and
Clear dramatic
I sang back, more of a
Murmur

So only she can
Hear

I can't say why
I just can't say why I just can't say
Say what else do you want to
Hear

From off stage sound of footsteps
Enter the Queen

She looks like Maye West on Acid just out of Alice in
Blunderland

She has that off with their head look glint in her one eye
The left being piratically black eye patched

How now `Felia .
How's this freak of a funeral flourishing?

Marlon thinks, those lines of hers are over rehearsed, their
down too pat

He's gonna be dead an gone
A father killed a mother
Stained
More will go to their
Graves
We're losing the
Plot
There will be not be tomb
Enough
To hide the

Slain

Sings Ophelia lady day Billie Holy Day-Eleanor Fagan-
Oya: Lester Young's lamenting sax is joined by
Miles's predatory trumpet: They're playing variations on
the tune Strange Fruit
In the dustbin makeshift coffin Scumbag shape shifts
into James Baldwin

CANTO 4

O some slumber party Rip, 20 mins 20 hours 20 months but
Twenty years
It won't wash (ington Irvine)
Says Mr. Fields walking where the leaves of Whitman's
grass don't grow no
More

That's gonna bomb bomb bomb

Sing we the Geeks Korus
Who are at
Best
A motley crew cut out of has beens, neardonewells, and
woebetides
We who are singing for our supper and hopefully breakfast
Too: have been in our tymes, the wells and tides the
hydrated crew who sailed with Odysseus (Odd U see Us),
do you get the
Clew?

He looks like and possibly is WC Fields played by
Orson Welles, he's bringing up the back

Where the dust and flies are conjugating

"They're a takin me for a why not orange New Jersey
 Looser
 cause there ain't no fool in
Hamlet
Don't give me that loneliness
Polonius
Chorus
He's no more a fool than
Thee
Gentle reader

I'm the dude who put the dick in
Bank
ole water closet
WC Fields
His self closely related in fact plumbed together at
Birth delivered by ole sister Caesarian her knife wielding
stomach slitting
Self with ole slight of Thomas
Crapper himself dr. of dissemination brother of dr.
Duchamp urinal r
mutt
*(this is all taking place at the back of the theatrical funeral
cortège)*

"Are we going to rehearse the crash in the cortège?"
Says a voice off stage
*(All voices off sound either like the nineteen forties voice of
the what's up, doc of bugs bunny
Or the nine teen forties voice of Olive Oil out of Popeye)*

"Ah Jesus. We're not going to wake him up to be dyed
again"
Says Widows Weeds played by Fred up Stirs sister[8]

"Haven't I've got to be dancin' at the Club Go
Go
By nine (said in a bad imitation Irish accent)
She lilts.

This unscripted remark causes WC Fields to choke with
unsolicited glee.

But wasn't it written by Doublin` Dublin up Joyced
James, who'd be brought over to squat at the edge of Holy
Wood and re right the wronged Ulysses bits? Odd you see
us
(this is a question to which at present an answer has not
been Un
covered)
Into the middle of this back end of the funeral adaption of
Hamed let, this least of vans
Guards
This lack of director and direction
Has been attached to the cart- theatre - hearse a smaller
littler less significant
One
It's a not big, but eight foot tall, barred cage you'd keep a
captured wild animal in.
At its top in faded gold lettering the words "hunger artist
can just be discerned, glinting in a sun setting for just that
purpose"

---

[8] Adele Astaire

Beneath those words ringing in our cir kussed ears is:
squatting in the cage, listening to a scrawly call of trumpet
playing strumpets is Saint Franzed Kafater sack clothed
and ash-ed and fasting
Looking like Johan the Baptist waiting for a Salome
sandwich.

CANTO 5

*Fe Leah (Ophelia played by Billy (never on) Holiday
Sings of
Thanatos and Eros (a little death a lot of love)*
By a grave stone called luck I let him fuck me
Rotten
In a coffin wherein he was coughin' I blew his holy
doppelgänging
Wad
Cum flew like confetti spattering hot white and dripping
from the inside of the garbage can
lids surrogate specular container
Triple orgasmed he looked like Hamlet played by
Scumbag, being B L Zee Bub (the anti-rapper for Gee Ho
Vas cultish
Mob)
Tell Lonliest Monk (thelonious to you) is amongst a bunch
of wannabe coffins piled up against the sawed oaks that
birthed them
Playing that black Steinway piano those beautiful black
digits fingering strange fruit
In reverberating reverse
Missing (the once thought) necessary note but never
missing the sacred lilt of lament
He played as I fucked the triple

Goddess

He kept the beat, sweating in the afternoons luminous
sunshine

The black cows in the day glow green field with their
young

Seduced by his sound gently lowing as the gnats hover
above the muddy pool, spinning

To his rhythms

I came to (my get me to a nunnery habit rucked about my
naked hips

My cowl sperm spattered) beneath the Druid tree

With the nailed on sign

Lands End not far

Teas ice creams deck chairs for hire

Previously As B L Z Bubbas buttocks were clenching and
he was about to cum in

My cathedral of orgasmic delights

My chapel of the best of the rest

My pit to his pen

Dulum dulum dulum

My clenching right hand on his writhed cheeks

Slipped into his left hand trouser pocket

Cash I thought despite the immanence of

Orgasm

Cash I thought is always a good

Thing

As we came clandestinely together like the good thief of
the

Night

Now pulling the cash out from under my

Cowl,

I discover it to be not notes of currency but notes to hymn

Self
I was suddenly hungry and picked a quince from the
Druid tree
And read the notes at first indifferently
Which ran exactly, like this

CANTO 6

Tell loneliest Monk ups the ante on the piano
Billy as Ophelia sing it like a blues sea
Chante Shante
[Imagine] Popeye and Olive Oil as Tristan and
Isolde
[Imagine] Diedre and Naoise as Bonny and
Clyde
Billie {Never on Sunday} Holliday sings the notes she
pounds in BL Zee Bub's pocket
Sing
So the plan is
Cutting off the fuel, by magnetically pulsing the food
carrying truck's engines
The People
Now desperately hungry an dis-
Armed
Lined up, at the soup kitchens
At the side of ex school busses with the blacked out
windows
They hold out their hands
But instead of soup
We instruct them to first cross those hands in prayer at the
wrist
They are then instantly miraculously immobilized by our
 priestly guardians

By a simple yet efficient process of binding with the holiest
Of
Duct tapes
Which they'd been told to bring with them (ha ha ha)
Oh duct tape most efficient of all binders!
It beats both rope and barbed wire!
It beats both rope and barbed wire!
The trucks are waiting for the recalcitrant
Ones
Swift and Dexterous, two part-time prison guards
Dressed like macho motorcycle
Cops with flat peaked caps, knee high leather boots and
Those riding pants that balloon out from the hips to the
Knee
Are wrapping us in black plastic sheeting
Securing the sheeting over our duct taped mouths
Then stacking us like cordwood into cargo
Holds
The docile; hand secured with duct tape
Board the blacked-out windows of the yellow ex school
Buses for them
Destination ultimatum
Conversation
War, Sir, we nnnnnnnneeeeeeeeeddddd
War
The indispensable condition for stabilizing
Society
Then even the incorrigible subversives
Are turned into social slaves
Allegiance requires a cause
Cause requires an enemy
The enemy that defines the cause
Thus, spoke BL Zee Bub from his smoked coffin

Hypnotized by his doppelganger brother *Jee Ho Vah*

CANTO 7

The oxen drawn staged funeral coach was pulled up in a
copse of
Oaks
The oxen freed of the yoke chomping grass edge of the
Stream
The camp fires of the sundowner acting troop flickering in
the
dusk
Food cooking ,bodies resting ,some rehearsing, singing, the
good wine
Flowing
Back of the Oakes breaking into the resting circle clothes
torn
Khloe mascara outlining doe eyes is a sort of Robin Hood
figure
Dressed like a boy but definitely and defiantly a
Girl,
Bow across her shoulder quiver on her back
Busted lip one eye
Black
Figure curves out of those robin the hood
Clothes
Blonde hair showing she could have lovers where ever she
Goes
It's Lady Gaga playing Sylvia Plath being Sycorax *
Thinks Marlon (Marlon Brando whose playing Sigmund
Freud)
Freud is here but he wasn't good looking enough and he
couldn't

Act so he's back writing film script for the production of
the Tempest
And Hamlet (if he gets to it) ; it appears Brando is
directing as well as starring and this
Time staring at the bruised Female Robbing the hood of all
its senses
Lady Gaga light up a cigarette, who else he thinks could
possibly play
Sylvia good looking poetry brained Plath who just has to be
the wicked wonderous
Witch of the Algerian past present future the very mommy
of recalcitrant
Caliban ... Sycorax

He, Brando looks at her, sees her as all three at once Gaga
Plath Sycorax
They drift In And out of each other's physiognomy like
bottled smoke like
Magic mushroom like mist in the shape shifting dust of
fucked-up faeries
Brand, who decided that Freud should look. Like Brando in
one eyed Jacks.
Is method acting Sigmund dressed as a cowboy and he's
trying to get to triple Gaga
To book her, and I bet try to bed her
But first he sprawl tumbles falls over the flung out de feats
of Euphoria and Goodness as handsome and freaky a pair
of thespian dykes to fall, flat face upon
Hey you, they say, their four pale blue eyes
immediately owning his outer and inner intellectual
Space
Hay hey sweet boyo they croon
he likes that it sounds like his mom and sister Coo cooing

ooô ing him in his age
Of Nebraska innocence
You need us in that film play Tempest cause
We got the goods
Shoot he groans still flat on his back their eyes his Milky
Way
So in Greek the root (Eu
meaning goodness happiness or
contentment
And eu(Phoria) the act of carrying reveal a more EFFORT
bound situation
The etymology suggests that goodness contentment and joy
Are states demanding persistence and active engagement
It don't just 'appen goodness, it gotta work, Like the sun
and renew itself
Each day
We're the gals for that
they say
Cool
says Marlon as Freud
Look, there goes Dawn after Dark
Holding hands with to her right
Constant Becoming and to
Her left Rehabilitating
Subjectivity
That's my casting my wardrobe and
Location
Tell them to screen test you
Asp
Then get back to me
I'm sure you'll be great
Their blue eyes fade away
Goodness and Euphoria are already on their way

He rolls up onto his haunches
This is early Marlon no weight gain
There she is against the moon
She got some fiddle player
Sucking up to her
Some guy called Hughes and cry

He'll be playing second fiddle
Soon I'll hew his cry
But as he goes to introduce himself
All Stetson tipped mam and that one cool-eye
Laconic beneath the brim
She begin to sing

Done give me that God created by
Man
In his own image
What a sorry and blasphemous caricature of the ever
unknowable
The unseen incorporeal,
Monotheistic Mother Fuckers that you
Be

Robin Hood suit or no Robin Hood suit
Bow or no bow quiver of arrows no quiver
Of arrows she's untouchable
She is so hot
Marlon's very mind begins to steam
Up
Sycorax features comes more concrete
There's the unmistakable sound of orphaned
Feet

CANTO 8

And am I the
Arrow
The dew that flies
Suicidal
At one with the
Drive
Into the red
Eye
The cauldron of
Morning
And out of those released
Ashes
Arise Phoenix's
Love bites
On Your choking
Throat

Chorus
Summary Of the plotless plot
We have a traveling band of players somewhere in 16th
century
Europe maybe
They have a coach that is a stage (a stage coach) and also a
hearse
Upon which they rehearse bits of Hamlet and bits of
Tempest to do with death dying
And dying to get laid in the coffin
They are carrying a coffin which is actually a large garbage
can with the heart 12 leafed
Lotus Chakra painted in sacred green on the inside of its lid
In the coffin. Is B L Zee Bub doppelgänger of *JeeHoVah* (a

narcistic monotheistic capitalist
Embarrassed at being linked with his doppelgänger and
paying the head of the troop and director and actor
Marlon Brando to funeralize his brother in a series of
burials that look like plays)
This is Unbeknownst to most of the cast who, know there
burying someone but not who
The plot is complicated by Scumbag being smuggled out of
jail in the garbage bin
And slid onto the traveling stage coach off a milk stand
early one morning in a Devine mix up,
So, Marlon signed Scumbag to play B L Zee Bub as long as
he kept his mouth shut And stayed
In the bin/coffin
Sigmund Freud was hired as a major a pall ing bearer but
he's not good looking enough he's too short and worst he
can't fucking act enough to save his Eda puss so now he's
screen writing the finale act
And Marlon playing Freud

CANTO 9

Location
 Lowkey's Bar beneath the bridge edge of the Styx
Aphrodite (Goddess of Love) is just back from trick or
treating and drawing on a camel cigarette and Heyoka
(Native American Contrary)
Are sitting at the bar having just been served pulque by
barkeep Thaw
All sleeveless shirt hammer tattooed biceps and blonde
dreads
Aphrodite wearing shades is looking like Faye Dunaway
but not in Bukowski's Barfly

212

More like Chinatown. Heyoka reversed black baseball cap
with the AIM logo printed on it, long braided hair eagle
feather tied, running down the back of Crow Dog pine
ridge Sundance t shirt tight black jeans, scarlet red
sneakers, looking like John Trudell in Smoke Signals
Whas goin on
Aphrodite
Well the editor just called in an said he needed the
Ending ...
Ending?
says Aphrodite
Yep
says Heyoka
Ending, do we do endings?
Not to my knowledge
We do episodes that finish when the actors are
Done
Well what ya gonna do
says Aphrodite
Well the stage coach funeral cortège with that bunch of
Nere do well players
Is headed this way
So let's get them up on the
Karaoke stage and tell 'em it's the
Final curtain
They got so many dead or dying already almost the only
one alive is fucking in the
Coffin
Says Heyoka
Err isn't he the one they've been paid to bury
Says Aphrodite blowing an amazing purple smoke ring up
into the rafters
Uh huh

Bee L Zee Bub old *Jee Ho Vah's* doppelgänger being
played by the one and only
Scumbag your wannabe lover

CANTO 10

They'd had to come in under the shelter of darkness
Muffled wheels, silence ruled to get them into Lowkey
Parking lot back of the bar down at Styx river side without
State security knowing they existed or where they went
Bedding Blankets stretched out camp fires glowing in the
dusk
On Your Marx (Karl to his friends) and his able assistant
Knows all the
Angles Engels preparing the Karaoke stage and
interviewing the chorus
Who had seen the advertisements for the chorus payment
food drink and shelter
For the night or Knights
Choristers Way wayward/CapRicious/Coned Verse/
DiffICult/Con Flicting/ContraDicTory
InConPatible/Peverse/Difficult/aggravating/pesky
Pestiferous/vexing/annoyance/exasperating
Etc.
Marlon as Sigmund Freud no sooner had they arrived went
looking for fac totem tab-U-
Tent where the actual king of Sigh Ko Sis was finalizing
The script, but he wasn't.
There was a note left on his Viennese walnut desk his dog
Total consciousness was gone too.
The note read
Dreamed I had my tongue cut out by Christian inquisition
And my brain fried by pouring red hot

214

Steel talumeds in my ears, so
Gone to see my sweetie Andreas Salome whose running
psycho kindergarten at the
Kremlin
Rough film script for dialogue and characters on the table:
Damn it I coulda' been a contender
Yours waterfront siggy

DIALOGUES: OBJECTS OF VENERATION BECOME
OBJECTS OF AVERSION
CHANT: PENANCES EXPIATIONS DEFENSE
REACTIONS PURIFICATIONS PSYCHICK FIXATIONS

It would be different if demons really existed but we know
like gods
They are only the product of the psychic powers of
humanity created from out of some
THING
PERSONS OR THINGS REGARDED AS TABOO MAY
BE COMPARED TO,OBJECTS CHARGED WITH
ELECTRICITY, THEY ARE THE SEAT OF
TREMENDOUS POWER TRANSMITABLE BY
CONTACT
DELUSIONAL DISORDER SAVAGE NEUROTIC MAJ
ICAL SUPERSTICION INHIBITED DEVELOPEMENT
He would not walk behind HER till the rising tide had
washed away every trace of her footsteps

CANTO 11

Note: lady day as Ophelia leaving the restroom on the way
to the karaoke stage Lowkey's bar edge of the Styx
Remember there are no rehearsals

Scribed in pink lipstick
On the mirror vanitas
Beneath the half-moon cut out
On Lowkey's outhouse door

Exiting the
Outhouse
Eleanora Fagan/Billie Holliday/Lady Day/hired to play
Ophelia is ear bent
To the sound of (issuing thru the magic wreathing mists of
morning
Vapor rising off the river)

Tell Only Us Monk masticating over
Strange fruit
His upright piano afloat
The raft of medusa
Moored in the middle of the Styx
In the shadow of the bridge
Beneath which is located
Lowkey's bar

Day of the Lady Ophelia, Eleonora; got me from the
nunnery
Via the good shepherd
Shake a spear at the cruel world today, plays
Monk; those fingers pulling lost rapture from the
Keys
Her voice tender the ghost of angel
Past future present
Singing about herself as though a shadow
Ophelia
Raped at ten

Sent to the good shepherd reform
School
Known for meeting out harsh punishment
For minor infringement
Raped again at 14
Arrested for solicitation
A little later at the log cabin
Club
.... told him I was a
Dancer
He said
Dance
I tried it
He said I
Stunk
Told him I could
Sing
I sang
The customers stopped
Drinkin'.

Arrested on my death bed in hospital
On narcotics charges
A cop in the room
They took my flowers love letters and
Record player away

When you come to find
Me
The next
Day
I had 750 bucks taped to my
Thigh

Full fathom five Ham(let) you led me
Astray

Done you worry 'yer pretty head none
Tho
I'm on my way back
Gonna sing till you
Pray

CANTO 12

Chorus
Up on the karaoke stage at Lowkey's hideaway bar and
club for out of work Deities
Lost and Flounders the Pursued Maimed and Fleeing; the
Innocent Guilty and Tossed;
The Orphans the Unknown the Unknowable; the Sunk the
Un Sorted the Sensitive;
Hypocrites Hypochondriacs and Hypnotists; Jugglers
severed Jugglers in Vain
Keepers of the Fire De Frocked Shaman Alcoholic Nuns;
Fools Knaves Villains Cross Dressers Not so Cross
Dressers Calm Dressers and Un Dressers

Parked center of Lowkey's karaoke stage the staged
coached carrier of theatre and funereally actors of Hamlet,
Tempest and a constant funeral are rehearsing upon a
A hearse
Marlon Branded by his name is playing Sigmund Fried
bought in by Queen Gertie
To *Un eadupus* hamlet's complex
But Siggys done a runner, runned off with sexy Sigh Ko
Sis

Leaving Marlon film script less on a direction to erewhon
All Bilged up with a possible mutiny as his
Bounty
But as Aphrodite remarks to Heyoka (They are sitting up at
the bar viewing the
Stage)
He's playing it perfectly as Sigmund Freud in frustrated
Lust with his Taboo
The Totem Witch Caliban s Momma, the one and only
Tempest bringer
Sycorax played as Sylvia Plath by Lady Gaga

"I believe old Sigmund is in love lust with the triple
Goddess aspect
1) Chant 2) Poetic 3)Wisdom of the Feminine "

Says a voice off
Sounds Like Jung when he was easily Freudian to me says
Aphrodite

Billie as Ophelia sweeps in just as
Lady Gaga Sylvia Plath Sycorax are warming up
Singing an aria to over prosperous preposterous Prospero

Song:
Oh tempestuous Tempest
Born
Almanac of
Disaster and planetary
Uncertainty
Jupiter and the
Full moon conjunction opposed
Venus

Which play are we in girls (sung ala Billy Bragg)
Whose play is this
We ain't gonna play
Prospero no more no

It's too late to find your
Prosperity Pros Perro

The moons off her
Moorings
Too late to get
Your
Sorry ass to shore
Chorus
As they're singing on your Marx (Karl to his friends)
religion is the opiate of the masses
Stenciled on his Hammered and Sickled logo`d torn t-shirt
he wears to drive cab for Hades (de) livery service
Walks on the stage with a sandwich board
Irish Nachos 4 .95 Corn Nuggets 380 The Bomb 595 Texas
Twister Nachos 595
Mozzarella sticks 380 Fried Pickles 3.80 Cheddar Crisp
380 Artichoke Spinach Dip 395
New item
Chicken strip / beer battered fish basket 8 25!

Shit says walk in another's shoes to plagiarized sexual
Deviant and slave who along
With shapeshifter god fool and transvestite whore priest
And cop croupier conman pimp soldier farmer philosopher
Bum had only volunteered to be the chorus on the promise
Of free food and drink
It's ok say on your Marx the chorus victuals are free

Just a spontaneous shout of joy emits from the chorus
It's echo seems to rock the coffin garbage can off the back
Of the staged coach knocking On Your Marx and his
Sandwiched bored over
And rolling and ratting off the stage

CANTO 13

As the coffin-garbage can rolls down the slight incline
Away from the karaoke
Stage toward the bar where Aphrodite and Heyoka are sat
Watching the goings on
The can, its shiny revolving sides burnished by the tall
tallow candles seems to have a sound system within it

Is that Scumbag In there playing ole BL Zee Bubba ?
Say Aphrodite
As she takes a shot of the trusty Pulque
You betcha
 Says Heyoka

Voice(s) issuing from the coffin/can
Which
Sounds like a combo of Howling
Wolf and Paul Robeson with Lenny the
Bruce on harmonica

Song:
Hu mill eeee a tion spread those feet
While we pat you down cuff you and throw you in that cell
No calls no nothing
Sit you there an look thru the peephole at you then slam it
Shut

Like I'm just a pariah fugitive running from your
Debts
The ubiquitous explorer, the observer of your
Mystery
The haunted traveler in the world of your
Phantoms
An ailing prophet. Roaming the cosmopolis of your
Schemes
You invade me Into your futile fascinations your holy
terrors your scenes for pious
Deliverance
Let us outa your confinement your solitary dismal
Dismissal, this cruel
Law for pitting the rich against the poor the lost and lonely
Enquirers agin the
Rest

Least let us Back to our sordid studios the place in our
Hearts where our pursued voices may
Take a moments respite
A refuge an island where our shipwrecked soul may find
Some
Delight
The dark ocean from which emerge bell towers like sturdy
Masts
You want to drag us down into your undulating
Crowd
To lose us in your clamoring multitude to, be drawn away
in The merciless current
Of your culture .....

The bin-coffin which has been moving in slo mow the
Candle light dazzling off its revolving surface as the song

222

Crescendo to a finish
Rolls right up to the feet of Aphrodite and Heyoka; the lid
Pops off and curves in a spiral spinning and slowly
Stopping, its inside lid a painting of the green 12 petal lotus
Heart chakra showing
Scumbag as Houdini as BL Zee Bubba is ejected half out of
The bin in his penitentiary orange
Jump suit manacled Hand to heel with a inquisitional
Garrote around his throat for good measure
On his back his eye running up the Split skirt seeing the ut
Of focus golden calf and impossibly beautiful thigh of The
Bar stooled sitting Aphrodite, up into the rafters where
Swinging in there ever open cage the twinned Ravens
Thought and memory smile down at him
Back on the stage the actors of Hamlet and Tempest have
Spontaneously
Coordinated with On your Marx and Knows All the Angles
Engels too
Billed all her Holy Days as Ophelia and Lady Gaga as
Sylvia Plath playing Sycorax
Are singing
It's Algerian Rai music led by Sycorax

As the coffin-garbage can rolls down the slight incline
Away from the karaoke
Stage toward the bar where Aphrodite and Heyoka are sat
watching the goings on
The can, its shiny revolving sides burnished by the tall
Tallow candles seems to have a sound system within it
Least let us Back to our sordid studios the place in our
Hearts where our pursued voices may
Take a moments respite
A refuge an island where our shipwrecked soul may find

Some
Delight
The dark ocean from which emerge bell towers like sturdy
Masts
You want to drag us down into your undulating
Crowd
To lose us in your clamoring multitude to, be drawn away
in The merciless current
Of your culture .....

The bin-coffin which has been moving in slo mow the
Candle light dazzling off its revolving surface as the song
Crescendoed to a finish
Rolls right up to the feet of Aphrodite and Heyoka; the lid
Pops off and curves in a spiral spinning and slowly
Stopping, its inside lid a painting of the green 12 petal lotus
Heart chakra showing
Scumbag as Houdini as BL Zee Bubba is ejected half out of
The bin in his penitentiary orange
Jump suit manacled Hand to heel with a inquisitional
Garrote around his throat for good measure
On his back his eye running up the Split skirt seeing the
Out of focus golden calf and impossibly beautiful thigh of
The bar stooled sitting Aphrodite ,up into the rafters where
Swinging in there ever open cage the twinned Ravens
Thought and memory smile down at him
Back on the stage the actors of Hamlet and Tempest have
Spontaneously
Coordinated with On your Marx and Knows All the Angles
Engels too
Billed all her Holy Days as Ophelia and Lady Gaga as
Sylvia Plath playing Sycorax
Are singing

It's Algerian Rai music led by Sycorax
Who as she steps to the front,
Takes on the form of white buffalo calf woman
Song sung in form of Lakota Rhythm eight-man drum beat
behind the woman's voices

Unisiiciyapi Wowacintanka Wowoohola Wayuonihan
Cantognake Icicupi Wowikape Waunsilape
Woohitike Cantewasake Canteyuke Wokasape[9]

Migratory bird flight
Cloud formation star alignment
Current drag
We don't have to have no compass sextant radio and patent
Log no clock and watch to
Watch

I am the star path navigator
Queen of the Cat Moran
Your star path navigator I am

Now we return our souls to the creator
As we stand on the edge of eternal darkness
Let our song fill the void
In order that followers may know
In the land of the night
The ship of the son
Is drawn by the grateful dead

As the queer choir is about

---

[9] Humility, Perseverance, Respect, Honor, Love, Sacrifice, Truth,
Compassion, Bravery, Fortitude, Generosity, Wisdom.

To sing the Buddha of delusion
Land such unreal delights
Aphrodite takes off her dark
Glasses
Slides them toward Thaw the barkeep,
And reaches down toward
Toward scumbag/ BL Zee Bubba is still aboard his trash
kan
Koffin
Is this where we sex in the coffin so he gets to rise
Again
Says Aphrodite
Marlon Branded the director playing Sigmund Freud (Who
wasn't good looking enough to play himself) and was
Reduced to being the scriptwriter who's done a Runner
With the inguen Sigh Ko's Sis (ter)
Nods
Heyoka says:
We can't do it I the coffin six foot under
And I think we've got to drop the mystery
Of the missing phallus bit
That's cool
Says Aphrodite reaching between the manacled chains
For the zipper
In scumbags/ BL zeebubbas orange penitentiary jump
Suit
There's a sudden loud crash

Chorus
What was that?
Sound of *jeehovah* pissed slamming them pearly gates
Sing Sycorax!

Adrian Frost is

S avant

E migrant

L over

F ool

AD Frost 7 14 47 St Ives Cornwall

very interesting

John Else

What's Right with Aging!
By
Dr. John F. Else

I agreed to write a chapter about aging and thoughts about death. I'm not sure I understand what is important about either of those things! While there have been many changes over the years, I haven't found any <u>great</u> changes in my life as I have aged, and I don't think about death much more than I have previously. But though they have not been huge changes, there have clearly been changes, so I'll discuss those.

I just turned 80 this year, but this week, as I sat in front of a medical appointment staff person to make a new appointment as I left my cardiologist's office, I gave the woman my name and she looked me up on her screen and said, "Your first name isn't John, is it?" I said, "Yes, it is." And she looked at the screen and read off my address and asked, "Do you live there?" I said, "Yes." She relaxed in her chair and said, "But you don't look 80! You look closer to 60!" I thanked her, and told her that other medical staff often say that when they look at my papers.

So, I guess I am quite fortunate, at least in my appearance. I recently met with a group of Sudanese young men, and in the course of the conversation, they asked whether I have children, and where they live. I said, "Yes, I have two and they both live here in the city. One is 52 years old and the other is 50." One man looked at me like I was an idiot—that I couldn't have children that old." I said, "Well, we were nearly 30 when we adopted them. I'm 80." Then he gave me a more amazing stare.

231

I grew up in a rural village of 780 folks in Nebraska. I have been a workaholic all my life. I lettered and was on the first team in basketball, track, and 8-man football all four years of high school. Whenever I wasn't in school or in athletic practice, I was working in my father's drug store (from the time I could calculate the change on a purchase)—both as a soda jerk and general sales person, and on Saturdays (fall and spring) and during the summers, I worked full-time and lived on my uncle's farm just outside of town. I bought all my own clothes once I started earning money. I attended University of Nebraska (during the years before Davaney, when we had regular losing football seasons) on a tuition scholarship and worked enough to pay all my other expenses.

During my employed career, I always did more than a job required. In fact, I fear that I was not a particularly good parent. Though I made real effort to spend time with my family, I don't think my first former wife (still a good friend) would agree. When we moved to eastern Iowa, she returned after one year to spend as much time as possible working on freeing a political prisoner whose defense/offense committee we had co-chaired for several years. We divorced (after 17 years) and I single parented the kids for 4 years, then took them with me for my sabbatical, 6 months in Zambia, then a couple months traveling on around the world, visiting friends in India, Indonesia (my son's god-parents), and Japan. That was before our stop in Hawaii, where the kids stayed in the hotel room watching children's TV for the first time in 8 months, while I went to the beach!

What is Especially Good About Retirement?

232

I retired in 2005, just two years after my open-heart surgery. The slowness of recovery and my distress about being unable to provide the level of energy I thought was essential for my work were the main reasons for my retirement at age 66.

I had prostate removal surgery two years after my retirement. The surgeon did robotic surgery, which was supposed to be safe, but I had internal bleeding afterwards (which he diagnosed incorrectly and prescribed blood thinner!), so had to undergo a second, regular surgery. As the surgeon helped move me from the gurney to the surgery table, he said, "You are really lucky. You get two surgeries for the price of one." I responded, "I would have preferred one good one!" And I would have! I have been impotent since then, which is no fun! But my wife has been very supportive and has "stayed in the game."

A year later, after two one-year episodes of failed replacement presidents, I was asked to return as interim president of the organization I founded. Even then, I had not yet realized that I should stay on rather than help select a new president. So, I helped to select another president whose failure extended over a longer period of time and essentially brought an end to the agency.

Grandparenting

A special wonder of retirement is being a grandparent. Like many, I have been a better grandparent than I was a parent. My wife, who had no interest in having children during her marriages, is a committed grandparent. When she retired, we moved to Florida, but the next summer, we decided to go to Omaha for the summer to assist with childcare for the three grandchildren of our two married children. At the end of the summer, Cathy said, "I don't want to go home." So, we moved to Omaha in October and have been here ever since. One of our children had another child, so we provided childcare three days a week until all four were in school full-time—one year ago. We are now "empty nesters," which has not been easy, especially for Cathy.

The grandkids are fun, most of the time—and the non-fun times are short, and we know they will soon be in their parents' homes, so it's OK. For several years, we provided family dinner for the 2 adult kids and their spouses or partners and the 4 grandkids. We've always enjoyed those events—except when we were living in an apartment that had no special space for the grandkids. So, the grandkids were often a hassle and the families left soon after dinner.

Then we bought a house with a full basement with a bedroom they used for toys and playing and a large play and TV room and a door to the outside fenced yard. That has been great. One time, the kids got an idea about digging a hole under the back fence and going through it. Nate, the youngest child, went through the hole, celebrated, and returned through the hole. Libby, the second-youngest, got halfway through the hole, but got stuck! She couldn't move. She got scared. She cried. Nate came in and quietly told his grandma that there was a problem, and she should come outside. When she found Libby stuck, she came back in and told his father. Nathan went out and decided the only way to get Libby out was to break off two pieces of the fence. He did that and she came out, greatly relieved.

Medical Changes

Retirement gives us more time for diagnosis and treatment of our many ailments. As noted, I had heart surgery before my retirement, then prostate surgery within two years. I've had other continuing medical issues, including some long-term issues: lower back pain and skin cancer. Since the late 1970s, I've treated the lower back pain via manipulation by Doctors of Osteopathic Medicine (DOs). My back has gotten better since my Omaha DO, who himself has, back pain problems, showed me exercises rather than perform some of the stressful (for the Doctor) manipulations himself. Two of the exercises have kept me in pretty good shape most of the time since he moved out of private practice to the VA clinic. Regarding skin cancer, I have a great dermatologist who examines me thoroughly every six months and freezes or cuts off all the pre-cancerous cells, so my skin cancer has been under pretty good control.

My general practitioner is an amazing man. He knows my medical history. He is concerned to find the source of each problem and identify a treatment for it. When I recently started having pain down one leg, he first sent me to physical therapy. But when that didn't produce any results in three weeks and the pain varied from one location to another, he decided it was a nerve problem, i.e., a nerve was being hit by the spine somewhere. He sent me to a pain management Doctor. I was hesitant, since I've read and heard so many negative things about pain management Doctors. It turned out the Doctor is an anesthesiologist who specializes in pain. He injects steroids into the spinal area to create a cushion between the spine and the nerve. I talked with one patient for whom it had been successful after one shot and another for whom it had required two. After one shot, much of the pain was gone, but I went back for a second shot a month later. It has now been five months, and I have very little pain. I am considering one more injection.

The other long-term concern is urinary incontinence. I have to take an expensive medicine and do frequent Kegels or I start leaking more and have to use more absorbent (and larger) pads. Then I go to a physical therapist who specializes in incontinence, and she got me into exercises and processes that nearly eliminate leakage. Yes!

Then, I suddenly got fibrillation, and that required a couple of expensive medications. Also, my hearing has gotten worse, so I've gotten hearing aids; it's hard to remember to put them in and take them out consistently and frustrating when you go forget, especially if you wear them in the pool, the shower, or the ocean.

The other factor in my aging is that starting about six months ago, when my energy level lowered. Unless I have some specific activity that fills the day, usually away from home, I usually lie down and rest for about an hour every afternoon. And I don't usually have the energy for work on my computer in the evenings—though if I have an important task, I find that energy.

Thus, though the problems multiply, all of them seem to be under control. So, my general feelings about my health is that I have outstanding doctors who keep me healthy, even if it requires more frequent visits and extra effort.

Using My Experience and Skills

After my 18 years of being a university professor and working extensively in Zambia and Zimbabwe and consulting in other African countries and in Eastern Europe, I founded and served as president of a non-profit agency that operated business development programs for low-income people statewide in Iowa, including a grant to work with refugees in the state. We also won a grant from the national refugee agency to provide technical services in business development, asset development, employment development, and other refugee programs. So, I had a wealth of experience in consulting with refugee agencies across the US for over 25 years. I had also worked in Zambia (6 months), Zimbabwe (2.5 years), supervised from DC a staff in Tanzania conducting a small business development program, and consulted in Lesotho, Swaziland, Malawi, Tanzania, Uganda, Russia, Poland, and Romania.

At first, I found retirement difficult. My second wife and I lived in Washington, DC, where she was still employed. I was used to working, and I wanted to continue to do active things as a volunteer. I made offers to several social agencies to provide free consulting or evaluations. None responded, but that may have been due to our newness to DC and that my work had not connected me with any local social agencies. I was not known to them—and in many cases, I didn't make my contacts with the directors of the agencies.

This changed quickly once we left DC. We first moved to our condo on the Gulf Coast of Florida. I got heavily involved in our condo's Board of Directors and in the development of a new agency focusing on small business development with low-income people. Then the next year we moved to Omaha. I have had a range of experiences in Omaha, including assisting multiple agencies submit, get incorporated, and obtain their tax-exempt status from the IRS. I have also gotten involved with two international non-profits: Legacy of Light, on whose Board of Directors I serve, install solar panels connected with electric lights on rural farm homes in El Salvador; and Wellsprings Mission digs wells in rural South Sudan.

My most major activity came after several years in Omaha. I got a call from a friend, the founder and Executive Director of Black Men United in Omaha. He told me that a South Sudanese man, whom I knew from meetings he had called, needed help with a non-profit that he had formed but had not been very successful to date. So, I called that man, and we met and discussed the situation with the organization—and I laid out the tasks where I thought I could help. This 48-year-old man had founded the non-profit with a vision to unite the various tribes of South Sudan (there are 64, of which at least 8-10 are present in Omaha) to learn English, become citizens, create fulfilling lives for their children, and participate actively in the community.

I was struck by the man's vision—a really great vision, as became increasingly apparent as I began working with the organization. However, the founder had limited education, primarily in the refugee camp. He then went to Community College for two years, then to an evangelical "college" for two years, after which he was ordained a minister. He formed a South Sudanese church, housed inside a mainline church facility, but my understanding is that it does not provide him with a salary. He works 10-12 hours per night, six nights a week, as a taxi driver, and his wife works full-time in a plastics factory. Consequently, he has no experience in an office environment (e.g., has never used a filing system), and no experience operating under the auspices of a board of directors or administering an organization. I am terribly perplexed by any related education or experience and deathly fearful that he may not be willing or receptive to learning.

I have learned much over time about South Sudan. I learned that the President of South Sudan was/is the Dinka (one of the two large tribes) General who led the independence revolution which culminated in an agreement for Independence if the citizens so voted. The Vice-President was a PhD of the Nuer tribe (the second large tribe—the two largest tribes constitute just over 50% of the population). Omaha was named the election location for South Sudanese to vote in the Independence election. Omaha has over 15,000 South Sudanese (25,000 in Nebraska). It is the largest population outside of Sudan. The election resulted in a clear vote for Independence, which occurred in 2011.

Many South Sudanese in Omaha returned to South Sudan both in preparation for Independence and immediately after Independence to contribute to building an effective government. However, when the Vice-President shared with the President his intention to oppose him in the next election, the President fired him and began a vicious civil war, killing hundreds of Nuer. So, the people in Omaha are severely divided among their tribes. There are about 32 Christian Churches in the Omaha area, each of them composed entirely of members of one tribe. They are hurt, angry, and untrusting of each other. This is the community which the founder had a vision for unifying for action and growth.

I learned that the agency was incorporated in 2013 and conducted several volunteer programs. It received tax exempt status in 2016. By 2017, it had no prospect of receiving grants. So, I agreed to write grants, something I have done repeatedly since 1964, when I was in the civil rights movement in Mississippi—and through my time in universities and as leader of a non-profit for 17 years. In the past year and a half, I have written nine grant applications. Two were rejected, four have been funded, and three are still under review (no action yet).

I also needed to give attention to the board of directors. The founder was also the volunteer Executive Director— plus he was the Chair of the board. He made all the decisions and then presented them to the board for approval. The board had no ownership of the organization's actions. I explained that the Executive Director could not serve on the board of a non-profit. So, he finally agreed to resign from the board, and he recruited a new board Chair, a man with bachelor and master degrees from Universities in the U.S., experience working in U.S. businesses, as well as operating U.S. non-profits., and then in leadership positions in South Sudan from 2005 until 2013.

So, we have been relatively successful in gaining funding for the organization. Our objectives now are to fulfill the commitments made in those grants. It is going to be difficult, but not impossible.

But there were also opportunities for failure. One of the first community service activities that arose in Omaha was serving on the board of directors of a refugee resettlement organization. The board consisted entirely of American born folks who in total had fewer years in refugee work than I. We agreed to recruit refugee members, interview them, share their resumes, and describe our perceptions. A date was set to vote on new members—the same process that had been followed for years.

During that meeting, the incoming Chair of the board said that he didn't want us to vote—that we should all have a chance to meet all these candidates. It seemed ethically improper to change the election procedure when we were voting on refugee members. I was angry and argued vigorously against that motion.

As interim Treasurer, I was invited to the Executive

Committee meeting the next week. When I arrived, I noted that there were two tall, large, African American men standing in the corner. We went through the normal agenda, then the Chair raised a new issue, asking me to resign from the board of directors. I refused to do that, since it was a decision that only the board as a whole could make. The chair asked me to leave and indicated that the two big men were in the room to escort me out. I said that I was not willing to be "escorted out"—that I would leave when everyone left. We all left, and the two men followed us out. I subsequently wrote a memo to all the board members describing what had happened, that I am a pacifist, a conscientious objector, so though I may have gotten angry in the last board meeting, I was not about to be violent in any way and was terribly confused about the presence of those "escorts."

I went to the office (where meetings are always held) for the next board meeting. The board meeting was not there. I was called to the phone, and told that the board meeting was being held at a restaurant several miles away. I proceeded to drive to the meeting, calling my wife in route so that she could help to calm me. When I arrived, a motion was made to terminate me from the board; it was voted on, with one abstention and my negative vote. I left the meeting. It is the first time in all my experience of teaching non-profit management in schools of social work in two universities that I had ever heard of such an action. It was a difficult event to adjust to, but with help from friends, I decided it was best that I was not a continuing part of such a board.

My Thinking About Death

First of all, I don't think about death much. When I do, it is the same as my thinking throughout my career, namely, (1) hoping that it will be as simple and peaceful as possible and (2) wanting to avoid inappropriate and unnecessary cost often spent on short survival. My father died of his third heart attack at age 51. My mother lived for many years with Alzheimer's. My sister died young of lung cancer and kidney failure. My brother is two years older than I and in much poorer health, having had several major issues, three severe strokes in 2 years and a failed heart valve. In the case of the strokes, his partner was fast with the aspirin, and he is extremely disciplined about his rehab routine. In the case of the failed valve, it was replaced in a now very simple procedure.

I have often thought about dying in a plane crash or in a fatal car accident. Many aren't so "fortunate." The central issue, for me and Cathy, is how to make the decision that it is time for us to die. How does one assure that they will be able to make that decision before they are no longer competent to make decisions? In case we are not, we both have long-term care insurance, but we are hopeful that we will not use it. Our desire is to make conscious personal decisions, when our lives, as we have always known them, is essentially over or likely to be over soon. Then, we will cease eating all food and drinking any liquids—with the approval of our family and friends. Our understanding is that, in most cases, death occurs within about two weeks. We believe this is the civil way to end our lives.

John Else grew up in Elm Creek, Nebraska. He received degrees from University of Nebraska in Lincoln, Yale University, University of Nebraska at Omaha, and Brandeis

242

University. He has had four careers: community organizer, academic, president of a domestic and international non-profit organization, and consultant. John has been married to two wonderful women. My first wife (for 17 years) is still an outstanding friend. My second marriage, which has lasted 35 years, is still functioning wonderfully. My first wife and I adopted two racially mixed infants, who have grown to be magnificent human beings and have made the three of us grandparents to four terrific kids.

Dave Buttgen

Aging with Grace

By

Dave Buttgen

I have rheumatoid arthritis. A very debilitating disease. It attacks and destroys my body's various linings by compromising my autoimmune defense system. Through the process of repairing those damaged parts, I've collected a large cadre of medical specialists: rheumatologist, cardiologist, orthopedic surgeons, and physical therapists. I was wrapping up my last rehabilitation session the other day whereupon my therapist (Gil) asked me where my *pain* level was on the 1 to 10 scale. After a little head scratching, I had to admit there was no *pain*. Of course, I'm sitting on a rather comfortable chair with no external simulation. I'm static – no movement. How could there be any *pain*? I'm at rest. With my typical sanctimonious arrogance, I replied, "Well, I guess I'm a little sore, but no *pain*. You need to change your definition parameters from *pain* to *sore*."

Pain brings life to a dead stop. Everything else becomes frivolous. Unimportant. All focus is on the debilitating *pain* and its relief. "It's gotta' stop; it's gotta' stop; it's gotta' stop." But the adjective *sore* is merely a distraction. At its worst, it merely slows me down. I don't move as fast. My hands don't work was well. The mind works, but the body can't keep up. But, I'm still a productive member of the team. I'm still in the game. Game of living. And, what exactly is meant by the word "living"? What does it mean to be alive?

247

It means I'm not dead! So "living" is that period from birth to death. AGING. I need to distinguish here between aging (as in *aging with grace*) and getting old. Old is the position, aging is the process. The process of hard-fought, small investments made over time determining our final position. The focus of this essay is to bring attention to aging: the universal and lifelong reality that from the moment of birth we grow old, that from our first breath we progress toward our last breath and every decision culminates into the old man or old woman we'll be. Aging is the dash on the tombstone, the little line that, in its progress from left to right, from the joy of birth to the sorrow of death, encapsulates a whole life. Aging comes with sorrows and joys and, in between them, are the responsibilities we choose to embrace or ignore.

I've written this with many tears—tears enough to surprise me and to show how deeply I feel about this subject, how much it has been a track playing in the background of my life, how much it remains a deep desire. These are tears of sorrow for wasted opportunities, tears of joy for evidences of undeserved grace, tears of hope. I am 74 years old—just about the oldest of the baby boomers (June 14, 1945). Behind me came 78 million plus boomers. Over 10,000 turn 73 every day. If you were to read the research, you would find that we boomers are a self-centered generation.

- *Likes:* working from home, anti-aging supplements, climate control
- *Dislikes:* wrinkles, Millennial sleeping habits, Social Security, insecurity
- *Hobbies:* low-impact sports, uber-parenting, wining and dining
- *Hangouts:* farmer's markets, tailgate parties,

backyards

- *Resources:* $2.1 trillion

What does it mean to get old as a baby boomer in America? It means a radical break with the mindset of our peers. Especially a break with the typical dreams of retirement. Most people don't die of old age, they die of retirement. "Retirement has always been a time when we see people withdraw from their roles," says Pauline Abbott, EdD, director of gerontology at the Institute of Gerontology, California State University, Fullerton. "During this risky time, some older people succumb to depression and a sense of meaninglessness. Part of the challenge of aging gracefully is that you have to continue to find things that are important to you, such as travel, spiritual pursuits, hobbies, new social groups, lifelong learning, or recapturing time with family."

Plan for purposeful activities before you retire. It should be a transition. It shouldn't be *Stop work one day and fall off a cliff.* It's time to follow where your passions lie. I read somewhere that half the people retiring in the state of New York die within two years. Does that mean retirement is a virulent disease, not a blessing? It doesn't have to be. But getting old is something everyone wants and yet fears.

Old has many frightening aspects: an aging body which is more susceptible to illness; declining strength; feelings of uselessness (especially after retirement); the loss of friends and loved ones through death; loneliness; feelings of alienation from one's children and grandchildren who are busy with other interests and pursuits; very often, financial concerns due to dwindling income; and, the reality of one's own death drawing nearer.

Sadly, our American culture does not esteem the elderly. We are a self-centered, utilitarian society. The younger generation often views the elderly as a financial burden and, if they require our care, as an interference in their pursuit of pleasure and success. This was most outrageously stated November 05, 1986 by then-Colorado governor, Richard Lamm. In a discussion of spiraling health care costs, he said terminally ill elderly people have "a duty to die and get out of the way." Most would be more polite, but the underlying attitudes are there.

Like the haves and the have nots, it's between those who are getting old and those who are getting old gracefully. You know, those beautiful oldsters who seem to get better and better with each passing year while others pass the blame onto others while griping their way through the few precious moments that are left and age without sublime *grace*. Well, take heart. We graceful oldsters aren't aging better; we're just aging smarter. The secret isn't necessarily in what we're doing. It's rather in what we aren't doing. Life expectancy continues to increase across the globe. It's true that aging brings hardships, but remember that we old-timers are survivors—a very select group.

As wisdom, resilience, and a mature perspective are often cited as the hard-won prizes of aging, actually just growing old in and of itself is an accomplishment. If you get to be a *senior citizen* you've survived lots of threats to your physical and psychological integrity. Those things that have affected other people who, by the way, are no longer with us. Through good luck or good genes or both, we the living have dodged fatal accidents, premature disease, and other things that kill the young. We are stronger, and get to live longer. Most people think that's a benefit. But, a generous dose of healthy denial can improve outlook in one's later years. We who do the best with aging aren't thinking much about getting older. We're not focusing on what's not working anymore. If I were to sit around mulling over the meaning of existence and how time is running out, I'd be building a scenario where I'm just getting old rather than aging with grace and dignity.

Getting old is rife with emotional landmines, including fears of losing one's independence or getting a serious illness. Aging gracefully isn't always easy, but attitude matters a lot. For some reason, society is obsessed with pointing out negative aspects of aging. But, don't get bogged down in all the hype about aging. Start obsessing about it and you can go nuts. We can't stop or slow the process down; the clock is going to tick away. Wrinkles reproduce themselves and lotions help but little. Sometimes we're surprised when everything works reasonably well. Yes, it would be wonderful to grow rich and stay healthy and enjoy every moment as we age, but that's not the lot of most of us most of the time.

In Nora Ephron's best-selling book[v], *I Feel Bad About My Neck*, she laments the sorry state of her 60-something neck: "Our faces are lies and our necks are the truth. You have to cut open a redwood tree to see how old it is, but you wouldn't have to if it had a neck," she writes. "Every so often I read a book about age, and whoever's writing it says it's great to be old. It's great to be wise and sage and mellow; it's great to be at the point where you understand just what matters in life. I can't stand people who say things like this. What can they be thinking? Don't they have necks?" With rueful humor, she writes about smoothing her face with Restylane and Botox, reading in large type, and grieving the deaths of beloved friends. Ultimately, Ephron concludes, "The honest truth is that it's sad to be over sixty."

Depression is a real threat among the old. Some drift into isolation, bitterness, and a sense of meaninglessness. Like it or not, all of us grow older ... all of us age. We can't avoid

251

it. So, what can we do to prepare ourselves for the slithering sludge of old age? Initially, you must know and ultimately accept that aging is not just a physical thing. Next, you must also know that the greatest achievements of your lives don't have to be limited to your younger days. History is full of people who have ignored or at least accepted that age is not a limiting factor in the equation of life:

- Laura Ingalls Wilder wrote her *Little House* series late into her 70s
- Peter Roget wrote *Roget's Thesaurus of English Words* at age 73 through 90
- Anna Mary Robertson "Grandma Moses" sold her first painting at 78, wrote her memoir at 95 and died at 101
- Frank McCourt authored *Angela's Ashes"* at the age of 65
- Ronald Reagan president at 70

Yes, we are all getting older. But, the one sure way to age gracefully – the sure one way to stay young – the one sure way to enjoy life, is to commit yourself to never retire from life!

We postpone acceptance of old age as long as possible because being old is deemed unattractive in a culture that worships athletic and beautiful young bodies. True, our society loves us, its senior members—as long as we don't look or act old. We begin aging at birth, so aren't there some preventive measures we can take to have a pleasurable old age? Any preparation is difficult because our capitalistic culture values productivity, and old people, instead of being seen as contributing, are considered a drain on resources. Gone are the times when villagers and family bestowed respectful dignity on the oldest among them as their walking encyclopedias of history and knowledge. Today, who needs us when they have Google? Yet our numbers are rapidly increasing, and we're living longer and have more needs. While each of us is a living snapshot of everyone's tomorrow, society's denial of old age makes us nearly invisible. If you wish to prepare wisely for your elderhood, upon seeing a hobbling old person, take a reverent moment to frame her or him as a prophetic holy icon of yourself someday. And do not treat aged strangers as if they were invisible. Stop to speak to them with a smile, and treat them with the esteem you wish to be given when your years advance and your body becomes stooped and disabled.

Aging changes everyone. If you live until you're 95 years old, you're probably not going to be living alone in a beautiful apartment and driving your car to the grocery store, or picking up your dry cleaning or walking a mile in the park. But if you know that ahead of time, it's much easier to manage it. To age gracefully, one needs to anticipate the changes that are inevitable. People who think rigidly do not do that. As they encounter the natural changes and health status that are part of aging, these things are experienced as negative and add a lot of stress and strain to their life. Rigid thinkers tend to get overwhelmed. They can't manage it, and they get depressed. Other people anticipate what's going to happen. It's more of a *Yes, I knew this was coming and I know I'll negotiate my way through it!* Even if you must limit your activities more than you might prefer, find and keep your stride, even though your pace may be slower than it was. It is quite all right to saunter a bit. Enjoy the trip. Just stay in good humor so others will enjoy the trip with you. Some enjoy joking about aging. But deep down inside growing old is something many dread. And fear. And are willing to do anything to avoid. Cosmeticians build multimillion-dollar businesses telling people how to do it. Exercise enthusiasts sell millions of dollars' worth of books and equipment to people telling how to do it. Health food manufacturers build huge businesses producing special foods promising it. And genetic scientists research ways to prevent it.

The art of graceful, dignified aging actually begins with affirmation. In a society that is consumed by body image and age avoidance, aging is a prospect that haunts and strikes fear into the hearts of many. Due in part to media portrayals of aging, some negative notions surrounding older people have resulted in thoughts and processes that dishonor the aging process by transmuting it into a belief that it must be avoided at all costs. It becomes increasingly difficult to form healthy opinions about the aging process when our media systematically promotes youth as the ideal human condition. In some cases, the anti-aging sentiment seen in movies, magazines, TV, and advertisements, older people—women and men alike—clamor to buy the latest and greatest anti-aging creams, potions, lotions and/or line up to undergo Botox injections, facelifts, and other surgeries promising to make us look younger and more vibrant. With so many equating aging with a sense of waning or decline, the process of growing older has become unjustly maligned and creates harmful and unnecessary fear as we try to escape the looming prospect of age. Aging is not a bad thing. In fact, nothing could be further from the truth. Aging is something to be celebrated. Old is a beautiful word, although often misunderstood and maligned. A house that has stood and sheltered for decades or centuries is honored. Antiques are valued. Even old cars draw attention because of their rarity and resale value. People filling their years can grow to become antiques (in the best possible use of the word) for their rarity, quality and ability to stand the test of time.

Aging gracefully and with dignity is a belief in the goodness of what you are experiencing.

Sue Ellen Cooper, 62, understands Ephron's dirge about "compensatory dressing" and obligatory hair-dye. "It's not disgraceful to mourn the loss of your beauty," Cooper says. "But it's going. So, you may as well do what you can and then forget it because there's so much more to life than how you look and what other people think of you." Almost a decade ago, Cooper started the Red Hat Society to celebrate women 50 and over. Red Hat now boasts 40,000 chapters in the U.S. and abroad. But Cooper admits that when she was younger, she harbored prejudice against older people. "When I would meet people, I'd think, "She probably wouldn't be a potential friend for me because she's 20 years older—just these things where we make a split-second judgment on appearance." Having met thousands of older women through the Red Hat Society, she has replaced the stereotypical thinking with a positive view of aging gracefully.

"A good life should be the aim of any person no matter what their age; living a good life is exactly how seniors can confidently ensure that they age with a radiant grace and venerable dignity."

But, as we all too well know, life will always have its stresses, from family to work to finances. It's unavoidable and can cause a barrage of health problems like

255

sleeplessness, depression, and heart disease. Some studies suggest stress can make you appear up to **10 years older**. But we, who are aging gracefully, have learned to manage our stress. Whether we do it through meditation, exercise, or just taking a couple minutes for ourselves.

The most effective way to de-stress our *golden* years is to stay away from negative people and avoid places and things that conjure up that downer mentality. I always try to be positive, and am thankful for what I have. Numerous studies have shown that positive people are less prone to mental decline and lead happier lives. As the **Huffington Post**[vi] reported, a 2011 survey found that older people who are happy have a 35 percent lower risk of dying than their unhappy peers. Positive people were also less likely to develop coronary heart disease, according to research done at **Harvard University**[vii].

It is vital that we do cheerfully what we can; to see a need and fill it; within the limits of our skills and abilities. Every day, we are building the house we will live in when old age comes. Some of us are building a beautiful palace. Some are building a dark prison. Perhaps you are building a house that will prove beautiful and comfortable through the long winter of your old age. You are decorating it tastefully, filling it with ornaments designed to bring pleasure and comfort in the days to come—deeds of gratitude and grace, acts of generosity and selfless love. On every wall, you are hanging pictures that are as meaningful as they are beautiful—warm friendships, mentoring and discipling relationships, children and grandchildren who know and love. They look down upon you to comfort, to cheer, to encourage. You have stockpiled supplies of grace to ensure you will be full and fed, faithful in the days of weariness. You have gathered great stores to fuel the fire, to keep it blazing brightly through the long winter days and nights. You have prepared a comfortable bed where you can lie and rest. As you draw your last breaths, you will be able to look from your bed to see those ornaments, those paintings, that lifetime of precious treasure, and you will know: You have lived a meaningful life.

Or perhaps you are building yourself a house that will prove little more than a cold, gloomy prison through the long winter of your old age. You are decorating it with ugliness and tastelessness; meaningless achievements; evil deeds; and self-righteous works. You are covering the walls with grotesque pictures; harmful friendships; broken relationships; children and grandchildren who are wanton and rebellious. They look down upon you to haunt you; to condemn you; to fill you with fear and sorrow. You have stocked sparse supplies to feed upon in the days of weariness, leaving you to chew on bitterness, regret, and a thousand empty vices. You have gathered little to fuel the fire, so it will burn low and extinguish, leaving you cold and miserable. You have prepared a bed of thorns where you will lie and desperately try to rest. As you draw your last breaths, you will look from your painful bed to see those awful ornaments, those dark paintings, that lifetime of piled regret, and you will know: your life was wasted and you have created a prison within your old age. The essence of entering that prison is loss. The possessions of those entering are confiscated. As they are stripped of clothing, lost too is their dignity. Elders experience this confiscation of dignity as well by examinations in doctors' offices and in various medical procedures. These losses increase as they age, as slowly hair color goes, and for some, hair itself. Bodily strength and agility are taken away, then teeth, eyesight and hearing. Painful losses of later years can include the fabulous freedom achieved at 16 of having a driver's license. At any time in aging comes a profoundly dreadful confiscation—loss of memory. When memories of loved ones, dear friends, adventures in life, one's work or profession are taken, the elderly are stripped naked to the bone.

What are you building? Are you building a palace or a prison? Are you building a place of joy, comfort, and **security**, or a prison of grief, sorrow and peril? Every day you are laying the bricks to your home. From childhood you have been decorating it. With each passing day you add new ornaments and you stock it—or don't stock it—for days to come. And as the winter of your life approaches, you will take up residence in the house you have built. So, I ask again, what are you building?

Life's memories can be beautiful. But many are not. Depression, losing friends and comrades, (the list goes on and on) can and does wear us down both physically and mentally. It is not healthy to obsessively relive our problems. We need to learn the appropriate lessons and try to live so that others, especially the young, are interested in what we have to say.

The best is yet to come is a cliché that is not self-evident to us aging baby boomers, but don't allow the advancing years to shrivel your enthusiasm, courage and fortitude.

Carry your years confidently, as a container filled with information, knowledge and hard-won wisdom. Though infirmity might compel you to live with limited activity, keep your heart and mind alive with enthusiasm. As we age, we experience an energy decline. The things we do now might take just a little longer. We have a tendency to allow interest and enthusiasm to decline. Be on guard.

There is one more thing I need to pass on: It's how you finish the race rather than how you start it. How something ends is crucial. People tend to remember how a life is finished better than they remember how they lived it up to that point.

Long ago the poet Robert Browning captured the gist of the autumn of life when he wrote: *"I'm growing fonder of my staff, I'm growing dimmer in the eyes, I'm growing fainter in my laugh, I'm growing deeper in my sighs, I'm growing careless of my dress, I'm growing frugal of my gold, I'm growing wise, I'm growing—yes—old."*

Browning captured much of the essence of aging, both the realities (which cannot be avoided) and the proclivities (which can and should be avoided). In so doing, he provided us with a valuable key to override our less-desirable natural tendencies during these years.

Early, middle and senior-middle age are the times to prevent ancient diseases such as prickly impatience, touchy irritability, moody grumpiness, pessimistic cynicism, criticism of youth, and sickly nostalgia for the good old days. In your early aging years, swear a vow never to indulge in any one of them. Strictly scrutinize your speech to guard against a sneak infection of even one debilitating virus. If you are already advanced in age and infected by one or more, then perform repeated, radical self-surgeries. As soon as you catch yourself complaining about anything, instantly yank out your griping like it was a painful rotten tooth. The best cure for old age's common bellyaching is taking the hard-to-swallow bitter pill of being your own critic. Honest self-examination is the best prophylactic for the old age pestilence of complaining about others. If you desire all your advanced years to be truly golden, develop the King Midas touch. Today, whatever your current age, begin touching everything in your life, including your health, with golden awareness and diamond gratitude. Use your mystical King Midas touch on those persons you love. If each day you turn the drab and dull tin of common things into gleaming treasure, you grow a habit that will make your ending years rich with contentment.

I expect that as you reflect on old age as an internment in prison you think this is a darkly misfortunate metaphor. I'm not surprised. Our American society, when speaking of the disadvantaged, tries to be "politically correct" and so for old age employs euphemisms like *senior* or *golden* years. The early years of growing older are for some indeed golden times for travel and hobbies. But the sand in the hourglass speedily drains out, and the golden years too often become the dark years of depression, pain, suffering and loss. Unfortunately, in advanced old age more dignity must be surrendered. Performing once-simple actions like bathing and other private bodily functions often requires the help of others. When these compromises or other undesirable needs like canes and walkers arise, a helpful medicine is prescribed by the Islamic Sufi saint *Jalal* ad-Din *Muhammad Rumi*, a Persian poet and Sufi master born 812 years ago in 1207, His writings have sold millions of copies in recent years, making him the most popular poet in the US:

Welcome difficulty into your life. Learn the alchemy that the moment you accept whatever troubles you've been given, the door opens. Alchemy, the secret chemistry of changing anything worthless into gold, opens the door for you to see that your embarrassing needs provide occasions for others to acquire the grace-filled gifts of being a caregiver.

The beautiful insight of Pierre' Teilhard, the French Jesuit priest, idealist, and philosopher is also a frightening challenge. The bottom line of this mystic wisdom of Teilhard is that each tribulation of aging becomes a divine homework assignment. With one such assignment being the daily routine of taking medications. Daily pill-taking can be compared to priests' obligation to pray the Divine Office at set times of the day. The elderly as well are obligated to take prescribed medications at specific times: sunrise, mid-morning or noon, evening and before going to bed. This daily taking of pills easily becomes disagreeable, so consider engaging in the spirituality of the Hopi Indians of the Southwest, who believe that all medicines should be taken with a prayer. It's wonderful how saying a mini-prayer can transform the bothersome obligation of taking pills.

The bathroom mirror sadly reflects back to us older people a seemingly unlovable body that threatens their love unions and friendships. Teilhard proposes hanging in place of the bathroom mirror a mystical mirror to encourage falling in love even in your old age. He says, *learn to love interior fragility and old age with its long shadows and ever-shrinking days ahead, and love diminishments and decline. A great and noble challenge it is to fall in love with your withered body and fading mind, and to love the dwindling days left in your life.*

In this essay I have tried to present a realistic image of old age, even if that meant some of its darker and depressive aspects. I close with 12 brief lines from Shakespeare's play "King Lear." At 80 years old, King Lear speaks to his daughter Cordelia, whom some think symbolizes his sprite spirit. Read slowly these beautiful lines:

No, no, no, no! Come, let's away to prison:
We too alone will sing like birds i' the cage:
When thou dost ask me blessing, I'll kneel down,
And ask of thee forgiveness: so we'll live,
And pray, and sing, and tell old tales, and laugh
At gilded butterflies, and hear poor rogues
Talk of court news; and we'll talk with them too,
Who loses and who wins; who's in, who's out;
And take upon's the mystery of things,
As if we were God's spies: and we'll wear out,
In a wall'd prison, packs and sects of great ones,
That ebb and flow by the moon.

Old age is a time for asking forgiveness, for gratitude and prayer, for singing and the telling of old tales. In the last years of our lives we become like God's spies as we enter into the mystery of things and laugh at the gossip of poor rogues who are still obsessed with who's in and who's out, who wins or loses at court, in the endless ebb and changes of the fickle old moon.

Starting that journey where one learns to age gracefully and with dignity is as simple as learning how to live a good life. What is a good life? It's happiness. Contentment. Pride. Confidence. Vigor. Vitality. Hope. Health. Responsibility. Awareness. Resilience. Optimism. Belief. A good life should be the aim of any person no matter what their age. It just so happens that living a good life is exactly how we seniors can confidently ensure that we age with a radiant grace and venerable dignity. Becoming older will inevitably come with various issues. For many of us

262

seniors, illness is a very real part of our lives, from dementia, being wheelchair-bound, or having to deal, like me, with painful rheumatoid arthritis. This essay is not about glossing over the debilitating conditions that may afflict us as we grow older. Rather it is about accepting the maladies our bodies experience and creating pragmatic solutions for the necessary health care and assistance required so that we can build a foundation to support our efforts to construct a happy and healthy life highlighted by a gentle, confident grace and self-affirming sense of dignity. Aging gracefully and with dignity is a belief in the goodness of what you are experiencing. It is tender, gentle affirmations that honor your being, the amazing journey of your life thus far, the countless experiences, moments of enlightenment, and beautiful memories that are the essential fabric of your being. Pay homage to yourself. Honor your age, your journey, and your being. Pay reverence to the life you have lived and, most importantly, believe in the beauty that lies ahead for you. The art of graceful dignified aging truly begins with affirmation. Honoring yourself, eschewing the foolish notions of aging put forth by society, and having conviction in the beauty of your journey will be the point at which you truly learn how to age with dignity, grace, and the kind of beauty that matters.

David D Buttgen was born in 1945. "I became one of the very first of the, soon to be known as, baby boomers. The first 17 years of my working career, was as an undertaker in Chicago and NW Arkansas. Received my Structural Engineering degree from the University of Arkansas in

1981. Worked for General Dynamics Corporation (which became Lockheed) for 23 years as an international liaison engineer for the F-16 fighter aircraft. My career transitioned into the wonderful world of 3-D modeling. During the course of that development, I worked with Sandia National Laboratories, NASA, MIT and Georgia Tech University. Retired in 2004. Went to Malawi, Africa to help identify production problems within the local village owned fish farms. I designed zero-cost ovens originally used to remove volatiles from soy beans so that they could be used as fish food. The ovens were also used as bakeries to help expand the village's business base. To help aerate the Tilapia ponds I developed, from spare bicycle parts, wind turbines. The turbines, during the winter season, were reversed so that water could be transferred from distant wells. I authored numerous training courses, quality improvement seminars and technical dissertations. *Aging with Grace* is my first non-technical essay."

End Notes

---

[i] "The Age Gap in Religion Around the World," Pew Research Center: Religion & Public Life, June 13, 2018 https://www.pewforum.org/2018/06/13/the-age-gap-in-religion-around-the-world/

[ii] Wikipedia: Flying Spaghetti Monster https://en.wikipedia.org/wiki/Flying_Spaghetti_Monster

[iii] The Unorthodox Pastafarian Church: Our Lady of Occasional Certitude
   https://www.facebook.com/UnorthodoxPastafarian/

[iv] Church of the Flying Spaghetti Monster
   https://www.venganza.org/

[v] *I Feel Bad About My Neck,*[v] (September 10, 2006 it was listed at #1 on The New York Times Non-Fiction Best Seller list)

[vi] https://www.huffpost.com/entry/happiness-long-life_n_1068209?guccounter=1
[vii]

https://www.hsph.harvard.edu/news/magazine/happiness-stress-heart-disease/